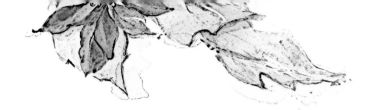

THE IDEALS TREASURY
OF BEST-LOVED
CHRISTMAS STORIES

THE IDEALS TREASURY OF BEST-LOVED CHRISTMAS STORIES

Julie Hogan, Editor

IDEALS PUBLICATIONS
A DIVISION OF GUIDEPOSTS
NASHVILLE, TENNESSEE

ISBN 0-8249-5861-6

Published by Ideals Publications
A division of Guideposts
535 Metroplex Drive
Suite 250
Nashville, Tennessee 37211
www.idealsbooks.com

Library of Congress CIP data on file

Color separations by Precision Color Graphics, Franklin, Wisconsin

Printed and bound in the USA by RR Donnelley, Willard, Ohio

10 9 8 7 6 5 4 3 2 1

Publisher, Patricia A. Pingry
Art Director, Eve DeGrie
Copy Editor, Melinda Rathjen
Permissions Editor, Patsy Jay

Book Design by Eve DeGrie

ACKNOWLEDGMENTS

DONOHUE, DINA. "Trouble at the Inn" from *Guideposts* magazine, January 1977, Carmel, NY. FINCH, ROSALYN HART. "The Red Mittens." Used by permission of the author. GOULD, JOHN. "Pioneers in Maine" from *Farmer Takes a Wife*. Copyright © 1945 by author John Gould. Published by William Morrow & Company. Used by permission of the author. MENOTTI, GIAN CARLO. *Amahl and the Night Visitors.* Copyright © 1986 by William Morrow and Company, Inc. Adapted from *Amahl and the Night Visitors* by Gian Carlo Menotti, copyright © 1951, 1952, 1980 by G. Schirmer, Inc. Used by permission of HarperCollins Publishers, Children's Books. OURSLER, FULTON. "Shepherds at the Back Door" from *The Greatest Story Ever Told* by Fulton Oursler. Copyright © 1949 by Fulton Oursler. Used by permission of Doubleday, a division of Random House, Inc. SANGSTER, MARGARET E. "What Christmas Brought a Stranger" from *Fifty Years of Christmas,* edited by Ruth M. Elmquist, Copyright © 1951 by Christian Herald Association. Published by Rinehart & Co., Inc. Used by permission of Christian Herald Association. SMITH, LILLIAN. "Tree-Shaking Day" from *Memory of a Large Christmas* by Lillian Smith. Copyright © 1962 and renewed 1990 by the author. Used by permission of W. W. Norton & Company, Inc. WARD, ANDREW. "The Christmas Feast" from *Out Here* by Andrew Ward. Published by Penguin Putnam, Inc. Copyright © 1991 by the author. WILDER, LAURA INGALLS. "Mr. Edwards Meets Santa Claus" from *Little House on the Prairie* by Laura Ingalls Wilder. Copyright © 1935, 1963 Little House Heritage Trust. Used by permission of HarperCollins Publishers, Children's Books.

Every effort has been made to establish ownership and use of each selection in this book. If contacted, the publisher will be pleased to rectify any inadvertent errors or omissions in subsequent editions.

CONTENTS

CHRISTMAS GIVING

THE GIFT OF THE MAGI

O. HENRY

One dollar and eighty-seven cents. And sixty cents of it was in pennies saved one and two at a time by bulldozing the grocer and the vegetable man and the butcher. Three times Della counted it. One dollar and eighty-seven cents. And the next day would be Christmas.

There was clearly nothing to do but flop down on the shabby little couch and howl. So Della did it. Which instigates the moral reflection that life is made up of sobs, sniffles, and smiles, with sniffles predominating.

While the mistress of the home is gradually subsiding from the first stage to the second, take a look at the home. A furnished flat at eight dollars per week. It did not exactly beggar description, but it certainly had that word on the lookout for the mendicancy squad.

In the vestibule below belonged to this flat a letterbox into which no letter would go, and an electric button from which no mortal finger could coax a ring. Also appertaining thereunto was a card bearing the name "Mr. James Dillingham Young."

The "Dillingham" had been flung to the breeze during a former period of prosperity when its possessor was being paid thirty dollars per week. Now, when the income was shrunk to twenty dollars, the letters of "Dillingham" looked blurred, as though they were thinking seriously of contracting to a modest and unassuming D. But whenever Mr. James Dillingham Young came home and reached his flat above, he was called "Jim" and greatly hugged by Mrs. James Dillingham Young, already introduced to you as Della.

Della finished her cry and attended to her checks with the powder rag. Tomorrow would be Christmas Day, and she had only one dollar and eighty-seven cents with which to buy Jim a present. She had been saving every penny she could for months, with this result. Twenty dollars a week doesn't go far. Expenses had been greater than she had calculated. They always are. Only one dollar and eighty-seven cents to buy a present for Jim. Her Jim. Many a happy hour she had spent planning for something nice for him. Something fine and rare and sterling—something just a little bit near to being worthy of the honor of being owned by Jim.

There was a pier glass between the windows of the room. A very thin and very agile person may, by observing his reflection in a rapid sequence of longitudinal strips, obtain a fairly accurate conception of his looks. Della, being slender, had mastered the art.

Suddenly she whirled from the window and stood before the glass. Her eyes were shining brilliantly, but her face had lost its color within twenty seconds. Rapidly she pulled down her hair and let it fall to its full length.

Now, there were two possessions of the James Dillingham Youngs in which they both took a mighty pride. One was Jim's gold watch that had been his father's and his grandfather's. The other was Della's hair. Had the Queen of Sheba lived in the flat across the air shaft, Della would have let her hair hang out the window some day to dry and mocked at Her Majesty's jewels and gifts. Had King Solomon been the janitor, with all his treasures piled up in the basement, Jim would have pulled out his watch every time he passed, just to see him pluck at his beard from envy.

So now Della's beautiful hair fell about her, rippling and shining like a cascade of brown waters. It reached below her knees and made itself almost a garment for her. And then she did it up again nervously and quickly. Once she faltered for a minute and stood still while a tear or two splashed on the worn red carpet.

On went her old brown jacket; on went her old brown hat. With a whirl of skirts and with the brilliant sparkle still in her eyes, she fluttered out the door and down the stairs to the street.

Where she stopped the sign read: "Mme. Sofronie. Hair Goods of All Kinds." One flight up Della ran, and collected herself, panting, before Madame, large, too white, chilly and hardly looking the "Sofronie."

"Will you buy my hair?" asked Della.

"I buy hair," said Madame. "Take yer hat off and let's have a sight at the looks of it."

Down rippled the brown cascade.

"Twenty dollars," said Madame, lifting the mass with a practiced hand.

"Give it to me quick," said Della.

Oh, and the next two hours tripped by on rosy wings. Forget the hashed metaphor. She was ransacking the stores for Jim's present.

She found it at last. It surely had been made for Jim and no one else. It was a platinum fob chain, simple and chaste in design, properly proclaiming its value by substance alone and not by meretricious ornamentation—as all good things should do. It was even worthy of The Watch. As soon as she saw it she knew that it must be Jim's. Twenty-one dollars they took from her for it, and she hurried home with the eighty-seven cents. With that chain on his watch Jim might be properly anxious about the time in any company. Grand as the watch was, he sometimes looked at it on the sly on account of the old leather strap that he used in place of a chain.

When Della reached home, her intoxication gave way a little to prudence and reason. She got out her curling irons and lighted the gas and went to work repairing the ravages made by generosity added to love.

Within forty minutes her head was covered with tiny, close-lying curls that made her look wonderfully like a truant schoolboy. She looked at her reflection in the mirror long, carefully, and critically.

"If Jim doesn't kill me," she said to herself, "before he takes a second look at me, he'll say I look like a Coney Island chorus girl. But what could I do—oh, what could I do with a dollar and eighty-seven cents!"

At seven o'clock the coffee was made and

the frying pan was on the back of the stove, hot and ready to cook the chops.

Jim was never late. Della doubled the fob chain in her hand and sat on the corner of the table near the door that he always entered. Then she heard his step on the stair away down on the first flight, and she turned white for just a moment. She had a habit of saying little silent prayers about the simplest everyday things, and now she whispered, "Please, God, make him think I am still pretty."

The door opened and Jim stepped in and closed it. He looked thin and very serious. Poor fellow, he was only twenty-two—and to be burdened with a family! He needed a new overcoat and he was without gloves.

Jim stopped inside the door, as immovable as a setter at the scent of quail. His eyes were fixed upon Della, and there was an expression in them that she could not read, and it terrified her. It was not anger, nor surprise, nor disapproval, nor horror, nor any of the sentiments that she had been prepared for. He simply stared at her fixedly with that peculiar expression on his face.

"Jim, darling," she cried, "don't look at me that way. I had my hair cut off and sold it because I couldn't have lived through Christmas without giving you a present. My hair grows awfully fast. Say 'Merry Christmas!' Jim, and let's be happy. You don't know what a nice—what a beautiful, nice gift I've got for you."

"You've cut off your hair?" asked Jim, laboriously, as if he had not arrived at that patent fact yet even after the hardest mental labor.

"Cut it off and sold it," said Della. "Don't you like me just as well, anyhow?"

Jim looked about the room curiously.

"You say your hair is gone?" he said, with an air almost of idiocy.

"You needn't look for it," said Della. "It's sold." She went on with a sudden serious sweetness, "Shall I put the chops on, Jim?"

Out of his trance Jim seemed to quickly wake. He enfolded his Della. For ten seconds let us regard with discreet scrutiny some inconsequential object in the other direction. Eight dollars a week or a million dollars a year—what is the difference? The magi brought valuable gifts, but that was not among them. This dark assertion will be illuminated later on.

Jim drew a package from his overcoat pocket and threw it upon the table.

"Don't make any mistake, Dell," he said, "about me. But if you'll unwrap that package you may see why you had me going at first."

White, nimble fingers tore at the string and paper. And then an ecstatic scream of joy; and then, alas, a quick feminine change to hysterical tears and wails, necessitating the immediate employment of all the comforting powers of the lord of the flat.

For there lay The Combs—the set of combs, side and back, that Della had worshiped for so long in a Broadway window. Beautiful combs, pure tortoiseshell, with jeweled rims—just the shade to wear in the beautiful vanished hair. They were expensive combs, she knew, and her heart had simply craved and yearned over them without the least hope of possession. And now, they were hers, but the tresses that should have adorned the coveted adornments were gone.

But she hugged them to her bosom, and at length she was able to look up with dim eyes and a smile and say: "My hair grows so fast, Jim!"

And then Della leaped up like a little singed cat and cried, "Oh, oh!"

Jim had not yet seen his beautiful present. She held it out to him eagerly upon her open palm. The dull, precious metal seemed to flash with a reflection of her bright and ardent spirit.

"Isn't it a dandy, Jim? I hunted all over town to find it. You'll have to look at the time a hundred times a day now. Give me your watch. I want to see how it looks on it."

Instead of obeying, Jim tumbled down on the couch and put his hands under the back of his head and smiled.

"Dell," said he, "let's put our Christmas presents away and keep 'em a while. They're too nice to use just at present. I sold the watch to get money to buy your combs. And now suppose you put the chops on."

The magi, as you know, were wise men—wonderfully wise men—who brought gifts to the Babe in the manger. They invented the art of giving Christmas gifts. Being wise, their gifts were no doubt wise ones, possibly bearing the privilege of exchange in case of duplication. And here I have lamely related to you the uneventful chronicle of foolish children in a flat who most unwisely sacrificed for each other the greatest treasures of their house. But in a last word to the wise of these days let it be said that of all who give gifts these two were of the wisest. Of all who give and receive gifts, such as they are wisest. Everywhere they are wisest. They are the magi.

TILLY'S CHRISTMAS

LOUISA MAY ALCOTT

"I'm so glad tomorrow is Christmas because I'm going to have lots of presents," said Kate, glowing with anticipation.

"I'm glad as well," Bessy chimed, "though I don't expect any presents but a pair of mittens."

It was Tilly's turn to speak, and she startled them with her words, "I'm very glad tomorrow is Christmas, even though I shan't have any presents at all."

These sentiments were spoken as the three little girls trudged home from school, and Tilly's words struck a chord of pity in the others. Kate and Bessy wondered how she could speak so cheerfully and be so happy when she was too poor to receive even the smallest of gifts on Christmas Day.

"Don't you wish you could find a purse full of money right here in the path?" asked Kate, the child who was going to have lots of presents.

"Oh, don't I! If I could keep it honestly, that is," said Tilly, her eyes glowing at the prospect.

"What would you buy?" asked Bessy, rubbing her cold hands and longing for her mittens.

"I've worked it all out in my mind," Tilly responded. "I'd buy a pair of large, warm blankets, a load of wood, a shawl for mother, and a pair of shoes for me. If there were enough left, I'd give Bessy a new hat so that she would not have to wear Ben's old felt one."

The girls giggled at that, but Bessy pulled the funny hat down over her ears and said she was much obliged but she would rather have candy.

"Let's look, and maybe we can find a purse. People are always going about with money at Christmastime. How do we know someone has not lost it here on this path?" said Kate.

So the three little girls went along the snowy road, looking about them, half in earnest, half in fun. Suddenly, Tilly sprang forward, exclaiming loudly, "I see it! I've found a purse!"

Kate and Bessy followed quickly, but sputtered with disappointment as they realized that there was no purse lying in the snow but only a little bird. It lay upon the snow with its wings spread and feebly fluttered, too weak to fly. Its little feet were benumbed with cold and its once bright eyes were dull with pain. Instead of a chipper song, it could only utter a faint chirp now and then as if pleading for help.

"Nothing but a stupid old robin. How maddening!" cried Kate, sitting down to rest on a nearby tree stump.

"I shan't touch it. I found one once and took care of it until it was well. The ungrateful thing flew away the minute it was able," said Bessy, creeping under Kate's shawl and pulling her hands up under her chin to warm them.

Tilly heard not a word. "Poor little birdie!" she crooned. "How pitiful you look and how glad you must be to see someone coming along to help you. Don't be frightened, dear. I am your friend." Tilly knelt down in the snow, stroking the bird with her hand and pity in her face.

It was only then that she realized Kate and Bessy were laughing.

"Don't stop for that thing," they chided. "Now come along. Let's continue looking for a purse before it gets too cold and dark."

"You wouldn't leave it to die!" cried Tilly. "I'd rather have the bird than the money we might find in a purse. After all, the purse would not be mine, and I would only be tempted to keep it. But this poor little creature will thank and love me for my trouble. Thank goodness I came in time."

Gently lifting the bird, Tilly felt its tiny, cold claws cling to her hand and its dim eyes brighten as it nestled down with a grateful chirp.

"Now I've a Christmas present after all," she said smiling. "I've always wanted a bird, and this one will be such a pretty pet for me."

"He'll fly away the first chance he gets and die anyhow," said Bessy. "You'd be better off not to waste your time with him."

"He can't pay you for taking care of him, and my mother says it isn't worthwhile to help folks that can't help us," added Kate.

"My mother said, 'Do to others as you would to be done to by them,' and I'm sure I'd like someone to help me if I were dying of cold and hunger. I also remember the little saying, 'Love your neighbor as yourself.' This bird is my little neighbor, and I'll love him and care for him, just as I often wish our rich neighbor would love and care for us," answered Tilly. She leaned forward slightly, breathing her warm breath over the tiny bird, who looked up at her with confiding eyes, quick to feel and know a friend.

"What a funny girl you are," said Kate. "Caring for that silly bird, and talking about loving your neighbor in that serious way. Mr. King doesn't care a bit for you, and he never will, though he knows how poor you are. So I don't think your plan amounts to much."

"I believe it, and I shall be happy to do my part," answered Tilly. "I must bid you good night now, and I hope you'll have a merry Christmas and receive lots of lovely things."

As she left her friends and walked on alone toward the little old house where she lived, Tilly's spirits began to sink. Suddenly, she felt so poor. Her eyes were filled with tears as she thought of all the pretty things other children would be finding in their stockings on Christmas morning. It would have been so pleasant to think of finding something for herself and pleasanter still to have been able to give her mother something nice. So many comforts were lacking with no hope of getting them. The little family was pressed enough to simply find food and firewood.

"Never mind, birdie," whispered Tilly. "We'll make the best of what we have and be

merry in spite of our lack. You shall have a happy Christmas, anyway, and I know God won't forget us, even if everyone else does."

Tilly stopped a moment to dry her eyes and lean her cheek against the bird's soft breast. The tiny creature afforded her much comfort, though it could only love her, not one thing more.

"See, Mother, what a nice present I've found," she cried, entering the house with a cheery face that was like sunshine in the dark room.

"I'm glad of that, dearie, as I have not been able to get my little girl anything but a rosy apple. What a poor little bird it is. Here, quickly, give the poor thing some of your warm bread and milk."

"Why Mother, this bowl is so full. I'm afraid you gave me all the milk," said Tilly, smiling over the nice, steaming supper that stood ready for her.

"I've had plenty, dear. Sit down and warm your feet. You may put the bird in my basket on this cozy flannel."

After placing the bird tenderly into the basket, Tilly peeped into the closet and saw nothing there but dry bread.

"Oh dear," Tilly exclaimed to herself, "Mother's given me all the milk and is going without her tea because she knows I'm hungry. I'll surprise her by fixing her a good supper while she is outside splitting wood."

As soon as her mother left the room, Tilly reached for the old teapot and carefully poured out a part of the milk. Then from her pocket, she drew a great, plump bun that one of the schoolchildren had given her. She had saved it for just this purpose. She toasted a slice of the bun and set a bit of butter on the plate for her mother to put on it. When her mother came in, she found the table drawn up in a warm place, a hot cup of tea ready, and Tilly and the bird waiting patiently.

Such a poor little supper, and yet such a happy one, for love, charity, and contentment were welcome guests around the humble table. That Christmas Eve was a sweeter one even than that at the great house, where light shone, fires blazed, a great tree glittered, music sounded, and children danced and played.

"We must go to bed early," said Tilly's mother as they sat by the fire. "We must save the wood, for there is only enough to last through tomorrow. The day after, I shall be paid for my work, and we can buy more."

"If only my bird were a fairy bird and would give us three wishes," Tilly said quietly. "How nice that would be! But the poor dear can give me nothing, and it is of no matter." Tilly was looking at the robin, who lay in the basket with his head under his wing, nothing more than a feathery little ball.

"He can give you one thing, Tilly," her mother said. "He can give you the pleasure of doing good. That is one of the sweetest things in life, and it can be enjoyed by the poor as well as the rich." As Tilly's mother spoke, she softly stroked her daughter's hair with her tired hand.

Suddenly Tilly started with surprise and pointed toward the window. "I saw a face—a man's face," she confided in a frightened whisper. "He was looking in. He's gone now, but I truly saw him."

Tilly's mother stood up and went to the

door. "Some traveler attracted by the light perhaps," she said.

The wind blew coldly, the stars shone brightly, the snow lay white on the field and the wood, and the Christmas moon was glittering in the sky; but no human person was standing within sight.

"What sort of face was it?" asked Tilly's mother, quickly closing the door.

"A pleasant sort of face, I think, but I was so startled to see it there that I don't quite know what it was like. I wish we had a curtain there," said Tilly.

"I like to have our light shine out in the evening, for the road is dark and lonely just here, and the twinkle of our lamp is pleasant to people as they pass by. We can do so little for our neighbors. I am glad we can at least cheer them on their way," said Tilly's mother. "Now put those poor, old shoes to dry and go to bed, dearie. I'll be coming soon."

Tilly went, taking her bird with her to sleep in his basket near her bed, lest he should be lonely in the night. Soon the little house was dark and still.

When Tilly came down and opened the front door that Christmas morning, she gave a loud cry, clapped her hands together, and then stood still, quite speechless with wonder and delight. There, near the stoop, lay a great pile of firewood all ready to be burned. There was also a large bundle and a basket with a lovely nosegay of winter roses, holly, and evergreen tied to the handle.

"Oh, Mother! Who could have left it?" cried Tilly. She stepped out to bring in the basket, and her mother, a few steps behind, stooped down to scoop up the bundle.

"The best and dearest of all Christmas angels is called 'Charity,'" Tilly's mother answered, her eyes welling with tears as she undid the bundle. "She walks abroad at Christmastime doing beautiful deeds like this, and never staying to be thanked."

It was all there—all that Tilly had imagined. There were warm, thick blankets, the comfortable shawl, a pair of new shoes, and best of all, a pretty winter hat for Bessy. The basket was full of good things to eat, and on the flowers lay a small note saying, "For the little girl who loves her neighbor as herself."

"Mother, I really do think my little bird is an angel in disguise and that all these splendid things came from him," said Tilly, laughing and crying with joy.

It really did seem so. As Tilly spoke, the robin flew to the table, hopped to the nosegay, and, perching among the roses, began to chirp with all his little might. The sun streamed in on the flowers, the tiny bird, and the happy child with her mother. No one saw a shadow glide across the window or ever knew that Mr. King had seen and heard the little girls the night before. No one ever dreamed that the rich neighbor had learned a priceless lesson from his poor, little neighbor girl.

And Tilly's bird was a Christmas angel, for by the love and tenderness she gave to the helpless little creature, she brought good gifts to herself, happiness to an unknown benefactor, and the faithful friendship of a little friend who did not fly away, but stayed with her until the snow was gone, making summer for her in the wintertime.

SHARING THE LOVE OF CHRISTMAS

❋ THE DEEPLY REWARDING SPIRIT OF GIVING ❋

Every good gift and every perfect gift is from above,
and cometh down from the Father of lights, with
whom is no variableness, neither shadow of turning.

—JAMES 1:17

What can I give Him,
Poor as I am?
If I were a shepherd
I would bring a lamb;
If I were a wise man,
I would do my part;
Yet what I can I give Him—
Give my heart.

—CHRISTINA G. ROSSETTI

Somehow, not only for Christmas,
But all the year through,
The joy that you give to others
Is the joy that comes back to you;
And the more you spend in blessing
The poor and lonely and sad,
The more of your heart's possessing
Returns to make you glad.

—JOHN GREENLEAF WHITTIER

I have always thought of Christmas as a good
time; a kind, forgiving, generous, pleasant time;
a time when men and women seem to open their
hearts freely, and so I say, God bless Christmas!

—CHARLES DICKENS

Every good gift and every perfect gift is from above,

He comes in the night!
He comes in the night!
He softly, silently comes,
While the little brown heads on the pillows so white
Are dreaming of bugles and drums.
Who tells him, I know not,
But he finds the home
Of each good little boy and girl.

—Author Unknown

Hang up the baby's stocking;
Be sure you don't forget—
The dear little dimpled darling!
She ne'er saw Christmas yet;
But I've told her all about it
And she opened her big blue eyes
And I'm sure she understood it—
She looked so funny and wise.

Write, "This is the baby's stocking
That hangs in the corner here.
You never have seen her, Santa,
For she only came this year;
But she's just the most blessed baby!
And now, before you go,
Just cram her stocking with goodies,
From the top clean down to the toe."

—Author Unknown

We three kings of Orient are;
Bearing gifts, we traverse afar
Field and fountain, moor and mountain,
Following yonder star.

Born a King on Bethlehem's plain,
Gold I bring, to crown Him again,
King forever, ceasing never
Over us all to reign.

Frankincense to offer have I,
Incense owns a Deity nigh.
Prayer and praising all men raising,
Worship Him, God most high.

Myrrh is mine, its bitter perfume
Breathes a life of gathering gloom;
Sorrowing, sighing, bleeding, dying,
Sealed in a stone-cold tomb.

Glorious now behold Him arise,
King and God and Sacrifice,
Alleluia, Alleluia,
Earth to heaven replies.

—John H. Hopkins

and cometh down from the Father of lights. . . .

FROM LITTLE WOMEN

LOUISA MAY ALCOTT

Really, girls, you are both to be blamed," said Meg, beginning to lecture in her elder-sisterly fashion. "You are old enough to leave off boyish tricks, and to behave better, Josephine. It didn't matter so much when you were a little girl, but now you are so tall, and turn up your hair, you should remember that you are a young lady."

"I'm not! And if turning up my hair makes me one, I'll wear it in two tails till I'm twenty," cried Jo, pulling off her net, and shaking down a chestnut mane. "I hate to think I've got to grow up, and be Miss March, and wear long gowns, and look as prim as a China aster! And it's worse than ever now, for I'm dying to go and fight with Papa. And I can only stay home and knit, like a poky old woman!"

"Poor Jo! It's too bad, but it can't be helped. So you must try to be contented with making your name boyish, and playing brother to us girls," said Beth, stroking the rough head with a hand that all the dish washing and dusting in the world could not make ungentle in its touch.

"As for you, Amy," continued Meg, "you are altogether too particular and prim. Your airs are funny now, but you'll grow up an affected little goose, if you don't take care. I like your nice manners and refined ways of speaking, when you don't try to be elegant. But your absurd words are as bad as Jo's slang."

"If Jo is a tomboy and Amy a goose, what am I, please?" asked Beth, ready to share the lecture.

"You're a dear, and nothing else," answered Meg warmly, and no one contradicted her, for the "Mouse" was the pet of the family.

The clock struck six and, having swept up the hearth, Beth put a pair of slippers down to warm. Somehow the sight of the old shoes had a good effect upon the girls, for Mother was coming, and everyone brightened to welcome her. Meg stopped lecturing and lighted the lamp, Amy got out of the easy chair without being asked, and Jo forgot how tired she was as she sat up to hold the slippers nearer to the blaze.

"They are quite worn out. Marmee must have a new pair."

"I thought I'd get her some with my dollar," said Beth.

"No, I shall!" cried Amy.

"I'm the oldest," began Meg, but Jo cut in with a decided, "I'm the man of the family now that Papa is away, and I shall provide the slippers, for he told me to take special care of Mother while he was gone."

"I'll tell you what we'll do," said Beth. "Let's each get her something for Christmas, and not get anything for ourselves."

"That's like you, dear! What will we get?" exclaimed Jo.

Everyone thought soberly for a minute, then Meg announced, as if the idea was suggested by the sight of her own pretty hands, "I shall give her a nice pair of gloves."

"Army shoes, best to be had," cried Jo.

"Some handkerchiefs, all hemmed," said Beth.

"I'll get a little bottle of cologne. She likes it, and it won't cost much, so I'll have some left to buy my pencils," added Amy.

"How will we give the things?" asked Meg.

"Put them on the table, and bring her in and see her open the bundles. Don't you remember how we used to do on our birthdays?" answered Jo.

"I used to be so frightened when it was my turn to sit in the chair with the crown on, and see you all come marching round to give the presents, with a kiss. I liked the things and the kisses, but it was dreadful to have you sit looking at me while I opened the bundles," said Beth, who was toasting her face and the bread for tea at the same time.

"Let Marmee think we are getting things for ourselves, and then surprise her. We must go shopping tomorrow afternoon, Meg," said Jo, marching up and down, with her hands behind her back and her nose in the air.

LITTLE PICCOLA

AFTER CELIA THAXTER

*I*n the sunny land of France there lived many years ago a sweet little maid named Piccola. Her father had died when she was a baby, and her mother was very poor and had to work hard all day in the fields for a few sous.

Little Piccola had no dolls or toys, and she was often hungry and cold, but she was never sad nor lonely. What if there were no children for her to play with? What if she did not have fine clothes and beautiful toys? In summer there were always the birds in the forest and the flowers in the fields and meadows—the birds sang so sweetly, and the flowers were so bright and pretty. In the winter when the ground was covered with snow, Piccola helped her mother and knit long stockings of blue wool. The snowbirds had to be fed with crumbs, if she could find any, and then there was Christmas Day.

But one year her mother was ill and could not earn any money. Piccola worked hard all the day long, and sold the stockings which she knit, even when her own little, bare feet were blue with the cold.

As Christmas Day drew near, she said to her mother, "I wonder what the good Saint Nicholas will bring me this year. I cannot hang my stocking in the fireplace, but I shall put my wooden shoe on the hearth for him. He will not forget me, I am sure."

"Do not think of it this year, my dear child," replied her mother. "We must be glad if we have bread enough to eat."

But Piccola could not believe that the good saint would forget her. On Christmas Eve she put her little wooden patten on the hearth before the fire, and went to sleep to dream of Saint Nicholas. As the poor mother looked at the little shoe, she thought how unhappy her dear child would be to find it empty in the morning, and wished that she had something, even if it were only a tiny cake, for a Christmas gift. There was nothing in the house but a few sous, and these must be saved to buy bread.

When the morning dawned Piccola awoke and ran to her shoe. Saint Nicholas had come in the night. He had not forgotten the little child who had thought of him with such faith.

See what he had brought her. It lay in the wooden patten, looking up at her with its two bright eyes and chirping contentedly as she stroked its soft feathers. A little swallow, cold and hungry, had flown into the chimney and down to the room and had crept into the

shoe for warmth. Piccola danced for joy, and clasped the shivering swallow to her breast.

She ran to her mother's bedside. "Look, look!" she cried. "A Christmas gift, a gift from the good Saint Nicholas!" And she danced again in her little bare feet.

Then she fed and warmed the bird and cared for it tenderly all winter long, teaching it to take crumbs from her hand and her lips and to sit on her shoulder while she was working.

In the spring she opened the window for it to fly away, but it lived in the woods nearby all summer, and came often in the early morning to sing its sweetest songs at her door.

CHRISTMAS, OR THE GOOD FAIRY

HARRIET BEECHER STOWE

"Oh, to think up presents for everybody!" said young Ellen Stuart, as she leaned languidly back in her chair. "Dear me! it's so tedious! Everybody has got everything that can be thought of."

"Oh, no!" said her confidential adviser, Miss Lester, in a soothing tone. "You have means of buying everything you can fancy, and when every shop and store is glittering with all manner of splendors, you cannot surely be at a loss."

"Well, now, just listen. To begin with, there's Mama, what can I get for her? I have thought of ever so many things. She has three card cases, four gold thimbles, two or three gold chains, two writing desks of different patterns; and then, as to rings, broaches, boxes, and all other things, I should think she might be sick of the sight of them. I am sure I am," said she, languidly gazing on her white and jeweled fingers.

"And then there are cousins Jane and Mary—I suppose they will be coming down on me with a whole load of presents; and Mrs. B. will send me something—she did last year; and then there are cousins William and Tom—I must get them something, and I would like to do it well enough, if I only knew what to get!"

"Well," said Eleanor's aunt, who had been sitting quietly, "it's a pity that you had not such a subject to practice on as I was when I was a girl—presents did not fly about in those days as they do now. I remember when I was ten years old, my father gave sister Mary and me a most marvelously ugly sugar dog for a Christmas gift, and we were perfectly delighted with it—the very idea of a present was so new to us."

"Dear Aunt, how delighted I should be if I had any such fresh unsophisticated body to get presents for! But to get and get for people that have more than they know what to do with now—to add pictures, books, and gilding, when the center tables are loaded with them now. I wish myself that I were not sick and sated and tired with having everything in the world given me!"

"Well, Eleanor," said her aunt, "if you really do want unsophisticated subjects to practice on, I can show you more than one family to whom you might seem to be a very good fairy, and where such gifts as you could give with all ease would seem like a magic dream."

"Why, that would really be worthwhile, Aunt."

"Look right across the way," said her aunt. "You see that building?"

"That miserable combination of shanties?"

"Well, I have several acquaintances there who have never been tired of Christmas gifts, or gifts of any other kind. I assure you, you could make quite a sensation over there."

"Well, who is there? Let us know!"

"Do you remember Owen, that used to make your shoes?"

"Yes, I remember something about him."

"He has fallen into a consumption, and cannot work any more, and he and his wife and three little children live in one room over there."

"How do they get along?"

"His wife takes in sewing sometimes, and sometimes goes out washing. Poor Owen! I was over there yesterday; he looks thin and wistful, and his wife was saying that he was parched with constant fever and had very little appetite. She had, with great self-denial and by restricting herself almost of necessary food, got him two or three oranges, and the poor fellow seemed so eager after them."

"Poor fellow!" said Eleanor, involuntarily.

"Now," said her aunt, "suppose Owen's wife should get up on a Christmas morning and find at the door a couple of dozen of oranges, and some of those nice white grapes, such as you had at your party last week. Don't you think it would make a sensation?"

"Why, yes, I think very likely it might; but who else, Aunt? You spoke of a great many."

"Well, on the lower floor there is a neat little room that is always kept perfectly trim and tidy; it belongs to a young couple who have nothing beyond the husband's day wages to live on. They are, nevertheless, as cheerful and chipper as a couple of wrens, and she is up and down half a dozen times a day, to help poor Mrs. Owen. She has a baby of her own about five months old, and of course does all the cooking, washing, and ironing for herself and husband; and yet, when Mrs. Owen goes out to wash, she takes her baby and keeps it whole days for her."

"I'm sure she deserves that the good fairies should smile on her," said Eleanor.

"But you ought to see her baby," said Aunt E., "so plump and good-natured, and always clean as a lily. This baby is a sort of household shrine; nothing is too sacred and too good for it."

"Why, did she ever tell you so?"

"No; but one day when I was coming downstairs, the door of their room was partly open, and I saw a peddler there with an open box. John, the husband, was standing with a little purple cap on his hand, which he was regarding with a mystified, admiring air, as if he didn't quite comprehend it, and trim little Mary gazing at it with longing eyes."

"'I think we might get it,' said John.

"'Oh, no,' said she, regretfully; 'yet I wish we could, it's so pretty!'"

"Say no more, Aunt. I see the good fairy must pop a cap into a window on Christmas morning. How they will wonder where it came from!"

"Well, then," continued her aunt, "in the next street to ours there is a miserable building, that looks as if it were just going to topple over; and away up in the third story, in a little room just under the eaves, live two poor, lonely old women. They are both nearly on to ninety. One of them is constantly confined to her bed with rheumatism, the other, weak and feeble, with failing sight and trembling hands, totters about her only helper; and they are entirely dependent on charity."

"Can't they do anything? Can't they knit?" said Eleanor.

"You are young and strong, Eleanor, and have quick eyes and nimble fingers; how long would it take you to knit a pair of stockings?"

"I!" said Eleanor. "What an idea! I never tried, but I think I could get a pair done in a week, perhaps!"

"And if somebody gave you twenty-five cents for them, and out of this you had to get food and pay room rent and buy coal for your fire, and oil for your lamp . . ."

"Stop, Aunt, for pity's sake!"

"Well, I will stop, but they can't; they must pay so much every month for that miserable shell they live in, or be turned out into the street. The meal and flour that some kind person sends goes off for them just as it does for others, and they must get more or starve, and coal is now scarce and high-priced."

"Oh, Aunt, I'm quite convinced, I'm sure; don't run me down and annihilate me with all these terrible realities. What shall I do to play a good fairy to these poor old women?"

"If you will give me full power, Eleanor, I will put up a basket to be sent to them, that will give them something to remember all winter."

"Oh, certainly I will. Let me see if I can't think of something myself."

"Well, Eleanor, suppose, then, some fifty or sixty years hence, if you were old, and your father and mother and aunts and uncles, now so thick around you, laid cold and silent in so many graves—you have somehow got away off to a strange city, where you were never known—you live in a miserable garret, where snow blows at night through the cracks, and the fire is very apt to go out in the old cracked stove; you sit crouching over the dying embers the evening before Christmas—nobody to speak to you, nobody to care for you, except another poor old soul who lies moaning in the bed—now, what would you like to have sent you?"

"Say no more, Aunt. I'll buy—let me see—a comfortable warm shawl for each of these poor women; and I'll send them, let me see—some tea—nothing goes down with old women like tea; and I'll make John wheel some coal over to them; and, Aunt, it would not be a very bad thought to send them a new stove. I remember the other day, when Mama was pricing stoves, I saw some, such nice ones, for two or three dollars."

"For a new hand, Ella, you work up the idea very well," said her aunt.

"Don't you think that it's right for those who have money to give expensive presents, supposing always, as you say, they are given from real affection?"

"Sometimes, undoubtedly. The Savior did not condemn her who broke an alabaster box of ointment—very precious simply as a proof of love—even though the suggestion was made, 'this might have been sold for three hundred

pence, and given to the poor.' I have thought he would regard with sympathy the fond efforts which human love sometimes makes to express itself by gifts, the rarest and most costly. "

Eleanor looked thoughtful; her aunt laid down her knitting, and said, in a tone of gentle seriousness:

"Whose birth does Christmas commemorate, Ella?'

"Our Savior's, certainly, Aunt."

"Yes," said her aunt. "And when and how was he born? In a stable! Laid in a manger; thus born, that in all ages he might be known as the brother and friend of the poor. And surely it seems but appropriate to commemorate his birthday by an especial remembrance of the lowly, the poor, the outcast, and distressed; and if Christ should come back to our city on a

Christmas day, where should we think it most appropriate to his character to find him? Would he be carrying splendid gifts to splendid dwellings, or would he be gliding about in the cheerless haunts of the desolate, the poor, the forsaken, and the sorrowful?"

And here the conversation ended. . . .

"What sort of Christmas presents is Ella buying?" said cousin Tom, as the waiter handed in a portentous-looking package, which had been just rung in at the door.

"Let's open it," said Will. "Upon my word, two gray shawls! And what's this? A great bolt of cotton flannel and gray yarn stockings!"

The doorbell rang again, and the waiter brought in another bulky parcel, and deposited it on the marble-topped center table.

"What's here?" said Will, cutting the cord. "Whew! a perfect nest of packages! oolong tea! oranges! grapes! white sugar! Bless me, Ella must be going to housekeeping!"

"Or going crazy!" said Tom, "And on my word," said he, looking out of the window, "there's a drayman ringing at our door, with a stove, with a teakettle set in the top of it!"

"Ella's cookstove, of course," said Will; and just at this moment the young lady entered, with her purse hanging gracefully over her hand.

"Now, boys, you are too bad!" she exclaimed, as each of the mischievous youngsters were gravely marching up and down, attired in a gray shawl.

"Didn't you get them for us? We thought you did," said both.

"Ella, I want some of that cotton flannel, to make me a pair of pantaloons," said Tom.

"I say, Ella," said Will, "when are you going to housekeeping? Your cooking stove is standing down in the street; 'pon my word, John is loading some coal on the dray with it."

"Ella, isn't that going to be sent to my office?" said Tom. "Do you know I do so languish for a new stove with a teakettle in the top, to heat a fellow's shaving water!"

Just then, another ring at the door, and the grinning waiter handed in a small brown paper parcel for Miss Ella. Tom made a dive at it, and staving off the brown paper, developed a jaunty little purple velvet cap, with silver tassels.

"My smoking cap, as I live!" said he. "Only I shall have to wear it on my thumb, instead of my head—too small entirely," said he, shaking his head gravely.

"Come, you saucy boys," said Aunt E——, entering briskly, "what are you teasing Ella for?"

"Why, do you see this lot of things, Aunt? What in the world is Ella going to do with them?"

"Oh! I know!"

"You know; then I can guess, Aunt, it is some of your charitable works."

Ella, who had colored to the roots of her hair at the exposé of her very unfashionable Christmas preparations, now took heart, and bestowed a very gentle and salutary little cuff on the saucy head that still wore the purple cap, and then hastened to gather up her various purchases.

But our story spins on too long. If anybody wants to see the results of Ella's first attempts at good fairyism, they can call at the doors of two or three old buildings on Christmas morning, and they shall hear all about it.

Yes, Virginia, There Is a Santa Claus

Francis P. Church

We take pleasure in answering thus prominently the communication below, expressing at the same time our great gratification that its faithful author is numbered among the friends of *The Sun*:

I am eight years old. Some of my little friends say there is no Santa Claus. Papa says, "If you see it in *The Sun*, it's so." Please tell me the truth, is there a Santa Claus?
—Virginia O'Hanlon

Virginia, your little friends are wrong. They have been affected by the skepticism of a skeptical age. They do not believe except they see. They think that nothing can be which is not comprehensible by their little minds. All minds, Virginia, whether they be men's or children's, are little. In this great universe of ours, man is a mere insect, an ant, in his intellect, as compared with the boundless world about him, as measured by the intelligence capable of grasping the whole of truth and knowledge.

Yes, Virginia, there is a Santa Claus. He exists as certainly as love and generosity and devotion exist, and you know that they abound and give to your life its highest beauty and joy. Alas! How dreary would be the world if there were no Santa Claus! It would be as dreary as if there were no Virginias. There would be no childlike faith then, no poetry, no romance to make tolerable this existence. We should have no enjoyment, except in sense and sight. The external light with which childhood fills the world would be extinguished.

Not believe in Santa Claus! You might as well not believe in fairies! You might get your papa to hire men to watch in all the chimneys on Christmas Eve to catch Santa Claus, but even if you did not see Santa Claus coming down, what would that prove? Nobody sees Santa Claus, but that is no sign that there is no Santa Claus. The most real things in the world are those that neither children nor men can see. Did you ever see fairies dancing on the lawn? Of course not, but that's no proof that they are not there. Nobody can conceive or imagine all the wonders there are unseen and unseeable in the world.

You tear apart the baby's rattle and see what makes the noise inside, but there is a veil covering the unseen world which not the strongest man, nor even the united strength of all the strongest men that ever lived could tear apart. Only faith, poetry, love, romance, can push aside that curtain and view and picture the supernal beauty and glory beyond. Is it all real? Ah, Virginia, in all this world there is nothing else real and abiding.

No Santa Claus? Thank God he lives and lives forever. A thousand years from now, Virginia, nay, ten times ten thousand years from now, he will continue to make glad the heart of childhood.

AN EMPTY PURSE

SARAH ORNE JEWETT

Little Miss Debby Gaines was counting the days to Christmas; there were only three, and the weather was bright and warm for the time of year.

"I've got to step fast to carry out all my plans," she said to herself. "It seems to me as if it were going to be a beautiful Christmas; it won't be like any I've spent lately, either. I shouldn't wonder if it turned out for the best, my losing that money I always call my Christmas money; anyway I'll do the best I can to make up for it."

Miss Debby was sitting by the window sewing as fast as she could, for the light of the short winter day was going, mending a warm old petticoat. Suddenly she heard a knock at the door; she lived in two upstairs rooms, and could not see the street.

"Come in!" she said cheerfully, and dropped her lapful of work.

"Why, if it isn't Mrs. Rivers!" she exclaimed with much pleasure.

The guest was a large woman, fashionably dressed. You would have thought that a very elegant blue jay had come to make a late afternoon call upon such a brown chippy-sparrow as Miss Debby Gaines. Miss Debby felt much honored, and brought forward her best rocking chair; and Mrs. Rivers seated herself and began to rock. Her stiff silk gown creaked as if she were a ship at sea.

"What are you doing—something pretty for Christmas?" she asked.

"It may be for Christmas, but it isn't very pretty," answered Miss Debby with a little laugh and shake of the head. "Tell you the truth, I was mending a nice warm petticoat that I don't have much use for; I thought I'd give it to old Mrs. Bean, at the poorhouse. She's a complaining, cold old creature, an' she's got poor eyesight an' can't sew, and I thought this would make her real comfortable. It's rather more heavy than I need to wear."

"I've been downtown all the afternoon, and it's so tiresome trying to get at anything in the stores," complained Mrs. Rivers. "They push you right away from what you want time to look over. I like to consider what I buy. It's a great burden to me trying to get ready for Christmas, and I thought I shouldn't do anything this year on account of my health. I've had large expenses this autumn. I had to buy new carpets and a new outside garment. I do like to see the pretty things in the stores, but they were so full of people and so hot and disagreeable this afternoon."

Miss Debby had picked up her petticoat and was holding it close to the window while she sewed on the button with firm linen stitches.

"I haven't been down the street for two or three days," she said. "You'll excuse me for going on with my work; it's most dark, and I'll be done in a moment; then we can sit an' talk."

"It does me good to come and see you once in a while," said Mrs. Rivers plaintively. "I thought I'd stop on my way home. Last year you had so many pretty little things that you'd been making."

"There aren't any at all this year," answered Miss Debby bravely. "It wasn't convenient, so I thought I'd just try having another kind of a merry Christmas."

"Sometimes I wish I had no more responsibilities than you have. My large house is such a care. Mr. Rivers is very particular about everything, and so am I." She gave a great sigh and creaked louder than before, but Miss Debby did not find the right sort of consolation to offer, and kept silence. "You enjoy having your pretty house," she ventured to say after a few moments; "you wouldn't like to do with as little as some." Mrs. Rivers shook her head in the dusk, and went on rocking.

"Presents aren't nothing unless the heart goes with them," said Miss Debby boldly at last, "and I think we can show good feeling in other ways than by bestowing little pincushions. Anyway, I've got to find those ways for me this year. 'Tis a day when we New England folks can seem to speak right out to each other, and that does us some good. Something gets in the air. I expect now to enjoy this Christmas myself, though I felt dreadful bad last week, saying to myself 'twas the first time I couldn't buy Christmas presents. I didn't know how interested I was going to get; you see I've made my little plans."

Then they talked about other things, and Mrs. Rivers grew more cheerful and at last went away. She always found Christmas a melancholy season. She did not like the trouble of giving presents then, or at any other time; but she had her good points, as Miss Debby Gaines always bravely insisted.

Early on Christmas morning Miss Debby woke up with a feeling of happy expectation, and could hardly wait to make her cup of tea and eat her little breakfast on the corner of the table before she got out her best bonnet and Sunday cloak to begin her Christmas errands. It was cloudy and dark, but the sunlight came at last, pale and radiant, into the little brown room; and Miss Debby's face matched it with a quiet smile and happy look of eagerness.

"Take neither purse nor scrip," she said to herself as she went downstairs to the street. There was nobody else stirring in the house, but she knew that the poorhouse would be open and its early breakfast past by the time she could get there. It was a mile or so out of town. She hugged a large package under her shawl, and shivered a little at the beginning of her walk. There was no snow, but the heavy hoarfrost glistened on the sidewalks, and the air was sharp.

Old Mrs. Bean was coming out of the great kitchen, and when her friend wished her a Merry Christmas, she shook her head.

"There ain't nobody to make it merry for

me," she said.

"I wish you a happy Christmas!" said Miss Debby again. "I've come on purpose to be your first caller, an' I am going to make you the only present I shall give this year. 'Tis something useful, Miss Bean; a warm petticoat I've fixed up nice, so's you can put it right on an' feel the comfort of it."

The old woman's face brightened. "Why, you are real kind," she said eagerly. "It is the one thing I've been wanting. Oh, yes, dear sakes! ain't it a beautiful warm one—one o' the real old-fashioned quilted kind. I always used to have 'em when I was better off. Well, that is a present!"

"Now I'm going, because I can come an' set an' talk with you any day, and today I've got Christmas work," and off Miss Debby went to the heart of the town again.

Christmas was on Tuesday that year, and she opened the door of a little house where a tired-looking young woman stood by an ironing table and looked at her with surprise. "Why, Miss Gaines!" she exclaimed, "where are you going so early?"

"I wish you a happy Christmas!" said Miss Debby. "I've come to spend the morning with you. Just through breakfast? No; the little girls are eating away yet. Why, you're late!"

"I didn't mean to be," said the young mother; "but I felt so tired this morning, and pretty sad, too, thinking of last year an' all. So I just let the children sleep. Nelly's got cold and was coughing most all night, and I couldn't bear to get up and begin the day. Mother sent for me to come over to spend Christmas, but I couldn't get the courage to start. She said she'd have

some little presents ready for the little girls, and now I'm most sorry I disappointed her."

"That's just why I'm here," said Miss Debby gaily, and with double her usual decision. "No, Nelly's not fit to go out, I can see; but you leave her here with me, an' you just get ready and take Susy and go. Your mother'll think everything of it, and I'll see to things here. Ironing? Why, 'twill do me good. I feel a little chilly, and Nelly and I can have a grand time. Now you go right off an' get ready, and catch the quarter-to-nine train. I won't hear no words about it."

So presently the pale, hard-worked young mother put on her widow's bonnet and started off down the street, leading bright-faced little Susy by the hand; and Miss Debby and her favorite, Nelly, watched them go, from the window. The breakfast dishes were washed and put away in such fashion that Nelly thought it quite as good as doll's housekeeping; and then, while Miss Debby ironed, she sat in a warm corner by the stove and listened to stories and to Miss Debby's old-fashioned ballads, which, though sung in a slightly cracked voice, were most delightful to childish ears. What a Christmas it was! Altogether there never was a happier Christmas Day, and the spirit of Christmas, of peace and goodwill, shone bright in Miss Debby's face.

She had started for home at dusk, just before it was time for young Mrs. Prender to get back, and was walking along the street, a little tired, but very happy.

"Why, it's only half past four o'clock now!" she exclaimed, as she passed the watchmaker's window. "I mean to go and see Mrs. Wallis a little while," and she quickened her steps.

She stopped here and there at the houses of other friends, forgetting in her happiness that she was empty-handed on Christmas Day, and everywhere she left a new feeling of friendliness and pleasant kindness. At one house she comforted a crying child by mending his broken top, and at another she knew just how to help a pretty girl to get ready for her Christmas party, and sat down and took off her big woolen gloves to alter the refractory dress, which had seemed impossible to be worn. She was like a good angel as she sat there, sewing and smiling and putting everybody's mind at ease.

It was late in the evening when this was finished, and she had had a long day; but she stopped, with great bravery, and asked to see the minister, just to tell him how thankful she was for his sermon on Sunday and wish him a happy Christmas. The minister had been a little discouraged for some reason, as ministers often are, and even Christmas kindnesses in the shape of welcome presents from his friends did not cheer him half so much as the sincerity and affection of Miss Debby's visit.

He watched the little figure go down the steps with tears in his eyes. So few persons could forget themselves to remember others as this dear parishioner could. It was worth living for, if one could sometimes help and refresh those who are the true helpers. He went back to his work in the study feeling like a better and busier man than when he had left it.

So Miss Debby came back to her little home again. The fire was out and it was all dark, but she went straight to her small rocking chair by the window and sat down to rest, and to thank the Lord for such a happy day. Though her purse was empty, her heart was full, and she had left pleasure and comfort behind her all along the way.

Presently she lighted her lamp, and then she saw on the table a great package with a note beside it; the note was from Mrs. Rivers.

"Something you said the other day," Miss Debby read, "made me feel differently about Christmas from the way I have before, and I am going right to work to try to make as many people happy as I can. And you must feel that my heart goes with these presents that I send you first. They are some of my own things that I liked, and I send them with love."

Miss Debby's face shone with joy. She had always liked Mrs. Rivers, but she had often pitied her a little; and now the note made her feel as if she had found a new friend in an old one. This was the way that Miss Debby's Christmas came to its happy end.

Down Pens

H. H. Munro (Saki)

Have you written to thank the Froplinsons for what they sent us?" asked Egbert.

"No," said Janetta, with a note of tired defiance in her voice; "I've written eleven letters today expressing surprise and gratitude for sundry unmerited gifts, but I haven't written to the Froplinsons."

"Someone will have to write to them," said Egbert.

"I don't dispute the necessity, but I don't think the someone should be me," said Janetta. "I wouldn't mind writing a letter of angry recrimination or heartless satire to some suitable recipient; in fact, I should rather enjoy it, but I've come to the end of my capacity for expressing servile amiability. Eleven letters today and nine yesterday, all couched in the same strain of ecstatic thankfulness: really, you can't expect me to sit down to another. There is such a thing as writing oneself out."

"I've written nearly as many," said Egbert, "and I've had my usual business correspondence to get through, too. Besides, I don't know what it was that the Froplinsons sent us."

"A William the Conqueror calendar," said Janetta, "with a quotation of one of his great thoughts for every day in the year."

"Impossible," said Egbert. "He didn't have three hundred and sixty-five thoughts in the whole of his life, or, if he did, he kept them to himself. He was a man of action, not of introspection."

"Well, it was William Wordsworth, then," said Janetta. "I know William came into it somewhere."

"That sounds more probable," said Egbert; "well, let's collaborate on this letter of thanks and get it done. I'll dictate, and you can scribble it down. 'Dear Mrs. Froplinson—thank you and your husband so much for the very pretty calendar you sent us. It was very good of you to think of us.'"

"You can't possibly say that," said Janetta, laying down her pen.

"It's what I always do say, and what every one says to me," protested Egbert.

"We sent them something on the twenty-second," said Janetta, "so they simply had to think of us. There was no getting away from it."

"What did we send them?" asked Egbert gloomily.

"Bridge-markers," said Janetta, "in a cardboard case, with some inanity about 'digging for fortune with a royal spade' emblazoned on the cover. The moment I saw it in the shop I said to myself 'Froplinsons' and to the attendant 'How much?' When he said 'Ninepence,' I gave him their address, jabbed our card in, paid tenpence or elevenpence to cover the postage, and thanked heaven. With less sincerity and infinitely more trouble they eventually thanked me."

"The Froplinsons don't play bridge," said Egbert.

"One is not supposed to notice social deformities of that sort," said Janetta; "it wouldn't be polite. Besides, what trouble did they take to find out whether we read Wordsworth with gladness? For all they knew or cared we might be frantically embedded in the belief that all poetry begins and ends with John Masefield, and it might infuriate or depress us to have a daily sample of Wordsworthian products flung at us."

"Well, let's get on with the letter of thanks," said Egbert.

"Proceed," said Janetta.

"How clever of you to guess that Wordsworth is our favorite poet,'" dictated Egbert.

Again Janetta laid down her pen.

"Do you realize what that means?" she asked. "A Wordsworth booklet next Christmas, and another calendar the Christmas after, with the same problem of having to write suitable letters of thankfulness. No, the best thing to do is to drop all further allusion to the calendar and switch off on to some other topic."

"But what other topic?"

"Oh, something like this: 'What do you think of the New Year Honor's List? A friend of ours made such a clever remark when he read it.' Then you can stick in any remark that comes into your head; it needn't be clever. The Froplinsons won't know whether it is or isn't."

"We don't even know on which side they are in politics," objected Egbert; "and anyhow you can't suddenly dismiss the subject of the calendar. Surely there must be some intelligent remark that can be made about it."

"Well, we can't think of one," said Janetta wearily. "The fact is, we've both written ourselves out. Heavens! I've just remembered Mrs. Stephen Ludberry. I haven't thanked her for what she sent."

"What did she send?"

"I forget; I think it was a calendar."

There was a long silence, the forlorn silence of those who are bereft of hope and have almost ceased to care.

Presently Egbert started from his seat with an air of resolution. The light of battle was in his eyes.

"Let me come to the writing table," he exclaimed.

"Gladly," said Janetta. "Are you going to write to Mrs. Ludberry or the Froplinsons?"

"To neither," said Egbert, drawing a stack of notepaper toward him. "I'm going to write to the editor of every enlightened and influential newspaper in the Kingdom. I'm going to suggest that there should be a sort of epistolary Truce of God during the festivities of Christmas and New Year. From the twenty-fourth of December to the third or fourth of January it shall be considered an offense against good sense and good feeling to write or expect any letter or communication that does not deal with the necessary events of the moment. Answers to invitations, arrangements about trains, renewal of club subscriptions, and, of course, all the ordinary everyday affairs of business, sickness, engaging new cooks, and so forth, these will be dealt with in the usual manner as something inevitable, a legitimate part of our daily life. But all the devastating accretions of correspondence incident to the festive season should be swept away to give the season a chance of being really festive, a time of untroubled, unpunctuated peace and good will."

"But you would have to make some acknowledgment of presents received," objected Janetta; "otherwise people would never know whether they had arrived safely."

"Of course, I have thought of that," said Egbert. "Every present that was sent off would be accompanied by a ticket bearing the date of dispatch and the signature of the sender, and some conventional hieroglyphic to show that it was intended to be a Christmas or New Year gift; there would be a counterfoil with space for the recipient's name and the date of arrival, and all you would have to do would be to sign and date the counterfoil, add a conventional hieroglyphic indicating heartfelt thanks and gratified surprise, put the thing into an envelope and post it."

"It sounds delightfully simple," said Janetta wistfully, "but people would consider it too cut-and-dried, too perfunctory."

"It is not a bit more perfunctory than the present system," said Egbert. "I have only the same conventional language of gratitude at my disposal with which to thank dear old Colonel Chuttle for his perfectly delicious Stilton, which we shall devour to the last morsel, and the Froplinsons for their calendar, which we shall never look at. Colonel Chuttle knows that we are grateful for the Stilton, without having to be told so, and the Froplinsons know that we are bored with their calendar, whatever we may say to the contrary, just as we know that they are bored with the bridge-markers in spite of their written assurance that they thanked us for our charming little gift. What is more, the Colonel knows that even if we had taken a sudden aversion to Stilton or been forbidden it by the doctor, we should still have written a letter of hearty thanks around it. So you see, the present system of acknowledgment is just as perfunctory and conventional as the counterfoil business would be, only ten times more tiresome and brain-racking."

"Your plan would certainly bring the ideal of a Happy Christmas a step nearer realization," said Janetta.

"There are exceptions, of course," said Egbert, "people who really try to infuse a breath of reality into their letters of acknowledgment. Aunt Susan, for instance, who writes: 'Thank you very much for the ham; not such a good flavor as the one you sent last year, which itself was not a particularly good one. Hams are not what they used to be.' It would be a pity to be deprived of her Christmas comments, but that loss would be swallowed up in the general gain."

"Meanwhile," said Janetta, "what am I to say to the Froplinsons?"

CHRISTMAS CUSTOMS

Mr. Edwards Meets Santa Claus

Laura Ingalls Wilder

The days were short and cold, the wind whistled sharply, but there was no snow. Cold rains were falling. Day after day the rain fell, pattering on the roof and pouring from the eaves.

Mary and Laura stayed close by the fire, sewing their nine-patch quilt blocks, or cutting paper dolls from scraps of wrapping paper, and hearing the wet sound of the rain. Every night was so cold that they expected to see snow next morning, but in the morning they saw only sad, wet grass.

They pressed their noses against the squares of glass in the windows that Pa had made, and they were glad they could see out. But they wished they could see snow. Laura was anxious because Christmas was near, and Santa Claus and his reindeer could not travel without snow. Mary was afraid that, even if it snowed, Santa Claus could not find them, so far away in Indian Territory. When they asked Ma about this, she said she didn't know.

"What day is it?" they asked her, anxiously. "How many more days till Christmas?" And they counted off the days on their fingers, till there was only one more day left.

Rain was still falling that morning. There was not one crack in the gray sky. They felt almost sure there would be no Christmas. Still, they kept hoping. Just before noon the light changed. The clouds broke and drifted apart, shining white in a clear blue sky. The sun shone, birds sang, and thousands of drops of water sparkled on the grasses. But when Ma opened the door to let in the fresh, cold air, they heard the creek roaring. They had not thought about the creek. Now they knew they would have no Christmas, because Santa Claus could not cross that roaring creek.

Pa came in, bringing a big fat turkey. If it weighed less than twenty pounds, he said, he'd eat it, feathers and all. He asked Laura, "How's that for a Christmas dinner? Think you can manage one of those drumsticks?" She said, yes, she could. But she was sober. Then Mary asked him if the creek was going down, and he said it was still rising.

Ma said it was too bad. She hated to think of Mr. Edwards eating his bachelor cooking all alone on Christmas day. Mr. Edwards had been asked to eat Christmas dinner with them, but Pa shook his head and said a man would risk his neck, trying to cross that creek.

"No," he said. "That current's too strong. We'll just have to make up our minds that Edwards won't be here tomorrow."

Of course that meant that Santa Claus could not come, either.

Laura and Mary tried not to mind too much. They watched Ma dress the wild turkey, and it was a very fat turkey.

They were lucky little girls, to have a good house to live in, and a warm fire to sit by, and such a turkey for their Christmas dinner. Ma said so, and it was true. Ma said it was too bad that Santa Claus couldn't come this year, but they were such good girls that he hadn't forgotten them; he would surely come next year. Still, they were not happy.

After supper that night they washed their hands and faces, buttoned their red-flannel nightgowns, tied their night-cap strings, and soberly said their prayers. They lay down in bed and pulled the covers up. It did not seem at all like Christmastime.

Pa and Ma sat silently by the fire. After a while Ma asked why Pa didn't play the fiddle, and he said, "I don't seem to have the heart to, Caroline."

After a longer while, Ma suddenly stood up. "I'm going to hang up your stockings, girls," she said. "Maybe something will happen."

Laura's heart jumped. But then she thought again of the creek and she knew nothing could happen. Ma took one of Mary's clean stockings and one of Laura's, and she hung them from the mantel shelf, on either side of the fireplace. Laura

and Mary watched her over the edge of their bedcovers.

"Now go to sleep," Ma said, kissing them good night. "Morning will come quicker if you're asleep."

She sat down again by the fire and Laura almost went to sleep. Then she heard Jack growl savagely. The door latch rattled and someone said, "Ingalls! Ingalls!" Pa was stirring up the fire, and when he opened the door Laura saw that it was morning. The outdoors was gray.

"Great fishhooks, Edwards! Come in, man! What's happened?" Pa exclaimed.

Laura saw the stockings limply dangling, and she scrooged her shut eyes into the pillow. She heard Pa piling wood on the fire, and she heard Mr. Edwards say he had carried his clothes on his head when he swam the creek. His teeth rattled and his voice shivered. He would be all right, he said, as soon as he got warm.

"It was too big a risk, Edwards," Pa said. "We're glad you're here, but that was too big a risk for a Christmas dinner."

"Your little ones had to have a Christmas," Mr. Edwards replied. "No creek could stop me, after I fetched their gifts from Independence."

Laura sat straight up in bed. "Did you see Santa Claus?" she shouted.

"I sure did," Mr. Edwards said.

"Where? When? What did he look like? What did he say? Did he really give you something for us?" Mary and Laura cried.

"Wait, wait a minute!" Mr. Edwards laughed. And Ma said she would put the presents in the stockings, as Santa Claus intended. She said they mustn't look.

Mr. Edwards came and sat on the floor by their bed, and he answered every question they asked him. They honestly tried not to look at Ma, and they didn't quite see what she was doing.

When he saw the creek rising, Mr. Edwards said, he had known that Santa Claus could not get across it. ("But you crossed it," Laura said. "Yes," Mr. Edwards replied, "but Santa Claus is too old and fat. He couldn't make it, where a long, lean razorback like me could do so.") And Mr. Edwards reasoned that if Santa Claus couldn't cross the creek, likely he would come no farther south than Independence.

So Mr. Edwards had walked to Independence. ("In the rain?" Mary asked. Mr. Edwards said he wore his rubber coat.) And there, coming down the street in Independence, he had met Santa Claus. ("In the daytime?" Laura asked. She hadn't thought that anyone could see Santa Claus in the daytime. "No," Mr. Edwards said; "it was night, but light shone out across the street.")

Well, the first thing Santa Claus said was, "Hello, Edwards!" ("Did he know you?" Mary asked, and Laura asked, "How did you know he was really Santa Claus?" Mr. Edwards said that Santa Claus knew everybody. And he had recognized Santa at once by his whiskers. Santa Claus had the longest, thickest, whitest set of whiskers west of the Mississippi.)

So Santa Claus said, "Hello, Edwards! Last time I saw you you were sleeping on a corn-shuck bed in Tennessee." And Mr. Edwards well remembered the little pair of red-yarn mittens that Santa Claus had left for him that time.

Then Santa Claus said, "I understand you're living now down along the Verdigris River. Have you ever met up, down yonder, with two little young girls named Mary and Laura?"

"I surely am acquainted with them," Mr. Edwards replied.

"It rests heavy on my mind," said Santa Claus. "They are both of them sweet, pretty, good little young things, and I know they are expecting me. I surely do hate to disappoint two good little girls like them. Yet with the water up the way it is, I can't ever make it across that creek. I can figure no way whatsoever to get to their cabin this year, Edwards," Santa Claus said. "Would you do me the favor to fetch them their gifts this one time?"

"I'll do that, and with pleasure," Mr. Edwards told him.

Then Santa Claus and Mr. Edwards stepped across the street to the hitching posts where the pack-mule was tied. ("Didn't he have his reindeer?" Laura asked. "You know he couldn't," Mary said. "There isn't any snow." "Exactly," said Mr. Edwards.) And Santa Claus uncinched the pack and looked through it, and he took out the presents for Mary and Laura.

"Oh, what are they?" Laura cried; but Mary asked, "Then what did he do?"

Then he shook hands with Mr. Edwards, and he swung up on his fine bay horse. And he tucked his long, white whiskers under his bandanna. "So long, Edwards," he said, and he rode away on the Fort Dodge trail, leading his pack-mule and whistling. Laura and Mary were silent an instant, thinking of that. Then Ma said, "You may look now, girls."

Something was shining bright in the top of Laura's stocking. She squealed and jumped out of bed. So did Mary, but Laura beat her to the fireplace. And the shining thing was a glittering new tin cup. Mary had one exactly like it.

These new tin cups were their very own. Now they each had a cup to drink out of. Laura jumped up and down and shouted and laughed, but Mary stood still and looked with shining eyes at her own tin cup.

Then they plunged their hands into the stockings again. And they pulled out two long, long sticks of candy. It was peppermint candy, striped red and white. They looked and looked at that beautiful candy, and Laura licked her stick, just one lick. But Mary was not so greedy. She didn't take even one lick of her stick.

Those stockings weren't empty yet. Mary and Laura pulled out two small packages. They unwrapped them, and each found a little heart-shaped cake. Over their delicate brown tops was sprinkled white sugar. The sparkling grains lay like tiny drifts of snow.

The cakes were too pretty to eat. Mary and Laura just looked at them. But at last Laura turned hers over, and she nibbled a tiny nibble from underneath, where it wouldn't show. And the inside of that little cake was white! It had been made of pure white flour and sweetened with white sugar.

Laura and Mary never would have looked in their stockings again. The cups and the cakes and the candy were almost too much. They were too happy to speak. But Ma asked if they were sure the stockings were empty.

Then they put their arms down inside them, to make sure. And in the very toe of each stocking was a shining bright, new penny! They had never even thought of such a thing as having a penny. Think of having a whole penny for your very own. Think of having a cup and a cake and a stick of candy and a penny. There never had been such a Christmas.

Now of course, right away, Laura and Mary should have thanked Mr. Edwards for bringing those lovely presents all the way from Independence. But they had forgotten all about Mr. Edwards. They had even forgotten Santa Claus. In a minute they would have remembered, but before they did, Ma said, gently, "Aren't you going to thank Mr. Edwards?"

"Oh, thank you, Mr. Edwards! Thank you!" they said, and they meant it with all their hearts. Pa shook Mr. Edwards' hand, too, and shook it again. Pa and Ma and Mr. Edwards acted as if they were almost crying. Laura didn't know why. So she gazed again at her beautiful presents.

She looked up again when Ma gasped. And Mr. Edwards was taking sweet potatoes out of his pockets. He said they had helped to balance the package on his head when he swam across the creek. He thought Pa and Ma might like them, with the Christmas turkey.

There were nine sweet potatoes. Mr. Edwards had brought them all the way from town, too. It was just too much. Pa said so. "It's too much, Edwards," he said. They never could thank him enough.

Mary and Laura were much too excited to eat breakfast.

"Don't make them, Charles," Ma said. "It will soon be dinnertime."

For Christmas dinner there was the tender, juicy, roasted turkey. There were the sweet pota-

toes, baked in the ashes and carefully wiped so that you could eat the good skins, too. There was a loaf of salt-rising bread made from the last of the white flour. And after all that there were stewed dried blackberries and little cakes. But these little cakes were made with brown sugar and they did not have white sugar sprinkled over their tops.

Then Pa and Ma and Mr. Edwards sat by the fire and talked about Christmas times back in Tennessee and up north in the Big Woods. But Mary and Laura looked at their beautiful cakes and played with their pennies and drank water out of their new cups. And little by little they licked and sucked their sticks of candy, till each stick was sharp-pointed on one end.

That was a happy Christmas.

TREE-SHAKING DAY

LILLIAN SMITH

Christmas began when pecans started falling. The early November rains loosened the nuts from their outer shells and sent them plopping like machine gun bullets on the roof of the veranda. In the night, you'd listen and you'd know IT would soon be here.

IT was not Thanksgiving. We skipped that day. At school, there were exercises, yes, and we dressed up like New England Pilgrims and play-acted Priscilla and Miles Standish and made like we had just landed on Plymouth Rock. But the truth is, the only Plymouth Rocks we saw in our minds were the black and white hens scratching round at the hen house. In those days, the Pilgrims and Thanksgiving did not dent the imaginations of little Southerners, some of whose parents wouldn't concede they had a thing to be thankful for, anyway. It was football that elevated the day into a festival—but that was later than these memories.

We eased over the national holiday without one tummy ache. Turkey? that was Christmas. Pumpkin pie? not for us. Sweet potato pie was Deep South dessert in the fall. We had it once or twice a week. Now and then, Mother varied it with sweet potato pone—rather nice if you don't try it often. Raw sweet potato was grated, mixed with cane syrup, milk, eggs, and spices, then slowly baked and served with thick unbeaten cream—plain, earthy, caloric, and good. But not Christmasy.

Pecans were. Everybody in town had at least one tree. Some had a dozen. No matter. Pecans were prestige. They fit Christmas.

And so you lay there, listening to the drip drip of rain and plop plop of nuts, feeling something good is going to happen, something good and it won't be long now. And you'd better sneak out early in the morning before your five brothers and three sisters and get you a few pecans and hide them. Strange how those nuts made squirrels out of us. Nothing was more plentiful and yet we hid piles of them all over the place. Of course, when there are nine of you and the cousins, you get in the habit of hiding things.

Our father chose the auspicious Monday to shake the trees. (Our weekly school holiday was Monday.) The shaking occurred after breakfast. He would stay long enough from the mill to get us well organized. I cannot remember a nonconforming breakfast on tree-shaking day; but on ordinary days, breakfast could be highly unpredictable. One never knew where rebellion would break out.

Our father customarily arose at five o'clock, drank a cup of coffee, walked to the mill, got things going there, got the logging train off to the woods, the mules off to the turpentine farm, got things going at the planing mill, the dry kiln, the shingle mill, and the big mill, got things going at the commissary, the office, the ice plant, the supply store which he owned half interest in, and the light plant and water works which he owned three-quarters interest in. Then, with everything going, he walked home to have breakfast with his children.

We were all in the dining room when he came back. A fire was sputtering in the fireplace if the day were cold, the bay window was fluttering with windy white curtains and sunshine and the nervous cage of the canary who was being stalked by one of the cats. The big long table was spread with a white Irish damask cloth—one of Mother's few self-indulgences. There were platters at each end of mullet roe (crisply fried) or smothered steak; there were three bowls of grits and four plates of thin light biscuits and two dishes of homemade butter and three pitchers of cane syrup scattered in between.

We each had our place. The two oldest sat on either side of our mother; the two youngest sat in high chairs on either side of our father; the others sat according to age in between. You took your turn sitting by Big Granny. You sat under duress, for not only was she wide, she had a habit of reaching over to your plate with her fork when both your hands were busy and spearing the morsel you had saved for last. On the walnut-paneled wall, behind the picture, was a small shelf on which lay the Bible and a thin peach-sprout

switch. The Bible was read every morning. The thin switch was used to quell whatever disorder was popping up among the younger ones.

We sat down. Our father read briefly from the Bible, closed it, rested his hand on it for a moment as though it gave him strength (and I think it did), then put it back on the shelf. He returned to the table, looked round at his nine, studied a face now and then as though it were new, beamed at Mother, then encouragingly asked for our verses. Each of us then said what we had gleaned from the Bible. The youngest always said, "Jesus wept." The next one always said, "God is love." The others were on their own. Verses began with the oldest and came down like a babbling stream to the youngest.

It was usually routine. But there were sudden uprisings. One morning, the six-year-old, when his turn came, calmly shouted "Jesus wept!" Silence. A scream from the youngest, "He tant have Thesus wept, he tant it's mine he tant he tant—" A scream from the four-year-old, "He tant have my Dod is love neider he tant he tant he tant—"

"Sssh . . . nobody's going to take your Jesus wept or your G—" He turned to the deviationist. "Why, Son," he asked gravely, "did you say your little sister's verse?"

"I'm tired," said Son. Mother looked at the tired one, who flashed his softest smile on her. When Father was not present it worked. No response now. He looked at Big Granny who could be fetched by it, too, but B.G. had seized the opportunity to spear a big piece of roe from an unguarded plate. Six-Year-Old swallowed hard. "I'm plumb wore out," he quavered.

Dissent more often came from the higher echelons. There was the summer when Age Fifteen decided it was time for subversion. He came close to bringing off a successful coup by the simple and highly effective device of teaching the Song of Solomon to one and all, even the littlest. He trained with cruel disregard of all the things we wanted to dream about or run and do. His sense of timing was superb; his dominance over us was complete, for we adored Age Fifteen, whose imagination never went to sleep. We would have loved to move into his mythic mind and live there forever with him. So we chanted our lines, as he ordered, and rechanted—quick, quick, he'd say, no wait, be ready, hook on now; and finally, we were zipping along like a chain reaction and he announced we were ready.

The morning came. He led off with "How beautiful are thy feet with shoes, O prince's daughter . . . thy navel is like a round goblet which wanteth not liquor . . . thy neck . . ." Each picked up his split-second cue and carried on, and it was climaxed by the two-year-old who piped out gaily, "Tay me wif flagons, tomfort me wif apples for I am thick of love."

And there was the time when one of the sisters—eleven years old that year—craving economy of effort and a smidge of excitement, specialized in the Begats. Each morning this pig-tailed plump daughter sang out to the dining room her story of begetting: "Enos lived ninety years and begat Cainan . . . And Cainan lived seventy years and begat Mahalaleel . . . and Mahalaleel lived sixty-five years and begat Jared," etc.

The parents could play it cool when they wanted to. For three mornings, they quietly ignored the giggles of the eight and the cousins, as Eleven-Year-Old begatted. But Eleven was too proud of her memory and her acrobatic skill with Semitic names and she loved the spotlight. The next morning she hung on to Genesis and begat and begat and begat. Her audience was hysterical. Then the two youngest, giggling wildly about what they could not comprehend, seized the chance to steal a biscuit before the blessing and promptly choked on their dual pleasures; and our father, beating alternately on two little wheezy backs, yelled (a measure reserved for near-disaster) "Stop it, you!"

Age Eleven, a thin-skinned if loquacious show-off, blushed and began to cry silently. And Big Granny, who had been having a ball spearing food off the platters along with the littlest ones, put a sausage on the conquered one's plate and told her to hush and eat, eating would make anything all right, and "What did the poor child do that was so wrong?" she shouted from her soapbox.

Our father looked at Mother. And Mother swiftly said, "Papa, please say the blessing—the other verses can wait until tomorrow."

But on tree-shaking day we were meek. We said proper verses, we bowed our heads for the blessing, we ate quickly, did not kick each other or yap at Big Grandma.

The moment we were excused from the table we ran to the linen closet for old sheets and spread them under the trees as our father directed. We got the baskets without being told. We were gloriously good. Even the little ones listened when Papa told them not to cry if the nuts hit their heads—anyway, they didn't need to get under the tree, did they? Of course, they needed to get under the tree, but they said yessuh and waved goodbye as Father walked down the tiled walk which led to the street which led to his office.

The one chosen to shake the tree first was usually the eldest. But now and then an ambitious underling snatched the honor away by bringing in wood for all twelve fireplaces without being told to or washing and polishing Mother's brougham and offering to drive her out to Cousin Lizzie's; or maybe he cleaned (with his sisters' help) all twenty-two lamp chimneys. . . .

Whoever won by fair or foul means the title of shaker of the tree did a pull-up to the first limb, hefted himself to the next, skittered into the branches and began to shake. Thousands of nuts fell until sheets were covered and thickening. Everybody was picking up and filling the baskets, except the little ones who ran round and round, holding their hands up to catch the raining nuts, yelping when hit, dashing to safety, rolling over the big boys' bird dogs, racing back.

Soon everybody was begging for more nuts on his side of the tree, for his turn shaking, for another basket.

This was how Christmas began for us.

THE LITTLE STRANGER

HANS CHRISTIAN ANDERSEN

Most children have seen a Christmas tree, and many know that the pretty and pleasant custom of hanging gifts on its boughs comes from Germany; but perhaps few have heard or read the story that is told to little children, respecting the origin of this custom. The story runs thus:

In a small cottage on the borders of a forest lived a poor woodcutter. He had a wife and two children who helped him. The boy's name was Valentine, and the girl was called Mary. One winter evening, with the snow and wind raging outside, this happy little family was sitting quietly round the hearth while they ate their supper of dry bread, when a gentle tap was heard on the window and a childish voice cried from without. "Oh, let me in, pray! I am a poor child, with nothing to eat, and no home to go to, and I shall die of cold and hunger unless you let me in."

Valentine and Mary jumped up from the table and ran to open the door, saying, "Come in, poor little child! We have not much to give you, but whatever we have we will share with you."

The stranger-child came in and warmed his hands and feet at the fire, and the children gave him the best they had to eat, saying, "You must be tired, poor child! Lie down on our bed; we can sleep on the bench for one night." Then said the little stranger-child, "Thank God for all your kindness to me!"

They took their little guest into their sleeping room, laid him on the bed, covered him over, and said to each other, "How thankful we are! We have warm rooms and a bed while this poor child has only heaven for his roof and the cold earth for his sleeping place."

When their father and mother went to bed, Mary and Valentine lay quite contentedly on the bench near the fire, saying, before they fell asleep, "The stranger-child will be so happy tonight in his warm bed!"

These children had not slept many hours before Mary awoke and whispered to her brother, "Valentine, dear, wake and listen to the sweet music under the window."

Then Valentine rubbed his eyes and listened. It was sweet music indeed, and sounded like beautiful voices singing to the tones of a harp.

O holy Child, we greet thee! bringing
Sweet strains of harp to aid our singing.

Thou, holy Child, in peace art sleeping,
While we our watch without are keeping.
Blest be the house wherein thou liest,
Happiest on earth, to heaven the nighest.

The children listened; then they stepped softly to the window to see who might be without. In the east was a streak of rosy dawn; and in its light, they saw children clothed in silver garments and holding golden harps in their hands. Amazed, the children were still gazing out of the window when a light tap caused them to turn around. There stood the stranger-child before them, clad in a golden dress with a gleaming radiance round his curling hair.

"I am the Christ child," he said, "who wanders through the world bringing peace and happiness to good children. You took me in and cared for me when you thought me poor, and now you shall have my blessing."

A fir tree grew near the house; and from this he broke a twig which he planted in the ground, saying, "This twig shall become a tree and shall bring forth fruit year by year for you."

No sooner had he done this than he vanished, and with him the little choir of angels. But the fir branch grew and became a Christmas tree, and on its branches hung golden apples and silver nuts every Christmastide.

Such is the story told to German children. Yet we may gather from this story the same truth which the Bible plainly tells us: that anyone who helps a child, it will be counted unto him as if he had indeed done it unto Christ himself. "Inasmuch as ye have done it unto the least of these, my brethren, ye have done it unto me."

CHERISHING CHRISTMAS TRADITIONS

❀ THE SPECIAL WAYS WE CELEBRATE THE SEASON ❀

Now that the time has come wherein
Our Savior Christ was born;
The larder's full of beef and pork;
The granary's full of corn.

As God hath plenty to thee sent,
Take comfort of thy labors;
And let it never thee repent,
To feast thy needy neighbors.

—AUTHOR UNKNOWN

Deck the halls with boughs of holly;
'Tis the season to be jolly.
Don we now our gay apparel,
Troll the ancient Yuletide carol,
See the blazing Yule before us,
Strike the harp and join the chorus;
Follow me in merry measure,
While I tell of Christmas treasure.

—WELSH CAROL

He comes in the night!
He comes in the night!
He softly, silently comes;
While the little brown heads
On the pillows so white
Are dreaming of bugles and drums.

He cuts through the snow
Like a ship through the foam,
While the white flakes around him whirl;
Who tells him I know not,
But he findeth the home
Of each good little boy and girl.

—AUTHOR UNKNOWN

Now Christmas is come, let's beat on the drum,

So now is come our joyful feast;
Let every soul be jolly!
Each room with ivy leaves is drest,
And every post with holly.

Though some churls at our mirth repine,
Round your brows let garlands twine,
Drown sorrow in a cup of wine,
And let us all be merry!

—George Wither

There's a jolly little fellow
Who comes riding into town
When the North Wind blows his trumpet,
And the snow comes dancing down;

In a coat of fur and ermine,
He is muffled to his chin,
And his face, whate'er the weather,
Always wears a pleasant grin.

O Fir-tree green!
O Fir-tree green!
Your leaves are constant ever,
Not only through the summertime,
But through the winter's snow and rime;
You're fresh and green forever.

—German Carol

He's a friend of all the children,
For he carries on his back
Gifts to make the bright eyes sparkle,
Safely stowed within his pack;

And they always hang their stockings
By the fireplace, because
Christmas Eve is sure to bring them
Presents from old Santa Claus.

—Author Unknown

Now Christmas is come,
Let's beat on the drum,
And call all our neighbors together.
And when they appear,
Let us make them such cheer
As will keep out the wind and the weather.

—Washington Irving

nd call all our neighbors together. . . .

THE NOEL CANDLE

CLEMENT C. MOORE

I t was Christmas Eve in Rheims, France, nearly five hundred years ago. The spires of the great cathedral towered high in the sky over a throng of people who had gathered in a square before the church, celebrating the joyous Noel. Laughing children darted through the crowd as groups of youths and maidens sang carols and danced to the music of a lute and tambourine. Everywhere faces shone with such happiness; it did not seem possible there could be, in all of Rheims, one sad and lonely heart.

Yet there were four. Three of them lived in a squalid old shed by the river. Though its outward appearance was dismal, the inside was neat and clean. Its one room served as living room, dining room, bedroom, and kitchen for three people; but the rough stone floor was carefully swept and the patched covers on the straw mattresses in the corner were spotlessly clean. A rough table, broken chair, stool, and rickety bench were the only furniture in the room. In a far corner stood a small charcoal brazier whose weak flame served not only to cook the meals but to warm the hut.

The one touch of beauty in the little room was supplied by a tiny shrine built on a shelf at the rear wall. A few field flowers in a bowl stood in front of it, and from the shelf hung a heavily embroidered scarlet sash which had once held a knight's shield.

A young woman was bending over a small spinning wheel, a boy of seven was setting the table with their few cracked dishes, and a girl a year or so older was stirring a kettle over the brazier. The lady, whose beauty shone through in spite of her ragged clothing, was Madame la Contesse Marie de Malincourt, and her son and daughter, Louis and Jeanne.

As she worked, the lady was thinking sadly of Christmas only a year before, when everything had been so different. Then she had lived in a great castle; and as on every Christmas Eve, she and her husband and children had gone down to the castle gate to greet the crowd assembled. The old, the ailing, and the poor would gather there; and the Malincourts would go into the crowd giving to each villager gifts of warm clothing, healing herbs, and food. Even Louis and Jeanne would give something from their own toys to the village children.

Then war had swept over their happy valley; the castle had been attacked and robbed. Lady Marie's husband had been led away in chains while she and the children had fled down a secret passageway out in the night and away to the village. She found it deserted, the villagers frightened away by the attackers.

During the months that followed, the three had wandered along the highway trading away their belongings, bit by bit, in return for food and lodging. Only one thing remained of their belongings—the cover of her husband's shield, which little Louis had brought from the castle that dreadful night. "Father gave it to me to keep until he comes back," he said. It was dear to all of them, for it was their only reminder of their father and the life they had shared together.

"Mother," said Jeanne suddenly, interrupting her mother's thoughts, "it is Christmas tonight."

"Yes, sighed Lady Marie, "but there will be no toys or sweets for you and little Louis."

"We don't need them," the children answered. "We have you, Mother, and we can keep Christmas in our hearts."

Their mother looked up at them and smiled. "Yes, though life is hard," she said, "we still have each other; and even though we miss your father, I'm sure there are others in Rheims tonight that miss their loved ones also. I just wish we had something to give the poor as we once did. . . ."

"Mother," Jeanne said excitedly, "I know something we can give." As she talked she picked up the small tallow candle from the table and hurried to one window of the hut.

"See," she went on, "I will put it on the sill and perhaps someone who passes, someone like ourselves, will be happier because of this little gift of light. There, see how it shines out on the snow," and she stood back to survey her work.

"You are a good child, Jeanne," said Lady Marie; then, smiling gently, she resumed her work.

Down in the great square, among all the lights and gaiety, was another sad heart. It beat in the breast of a little lad of nine, a boy in ragged clothes whose bare feet were thrust into clumsy wooden clogs. He was utterly alone in the world—without money or friends—cold, hungry, and miserable. When he tried to tell his story to some of the milling people around him, no one took any interest in him, other than to frown at him or elbow him out of the way.

At last, in utter despair, he began to tramp the streets, stopping now and then to gaze at the splendid houses and to seek help. But there was no welcome for the poor, lonely child.

It was dark in the streets of Rheims now, and the air was growing colder; but the little child trampled on, trying desperately to find shelter before the night closed in. At last, far off down by the river, he saw a tiny gleam of light appear suddenly at a window, and he hurried toward it. As he neared, the boy saw it was only a small tallow candle at the window of the poorest hut in all Rheims; but the steady light brought a sudden glow to his heart and he ran forward and knocked at the door.

It was quickly opened by a little girl, and at once two other people rose to greet him. In another moment he found himself seated on a stool beside the charcoal brazier. The little girl was warming one of his cold hands in her palms, while her brother was holding the other; and a beautiful woman, kneeling at his feet, drew off the wooden shoes and rubbed his icy feet. When he was thoroughly warmed, the little girl dished up into three bowls and a cracked cup the stew which had been simmering on the fire. There was only a little of it, but she passed the fullest bowl to the stranger.

After a word of blessing, they ate their stew and never had the thick soup tasted so rich and so satisfying. As they finished, a sudden flowing light filled the room, greater than the brightness of a thousand candles. There was a sound of angel voices, and the stranger had grown so radiant they could hardly bear to look at him.

"Thou, with thy little candle, have lighted the Christ child on his way to Heaven," said their guest, his hand on the door latch. "This night your dearest prayer shall be answered," and in another instant he was gone.

The countess and her children fell to their knees and prayed, and there they still were many minutes later when a knight in armor gently pushed open the door and entered the hut.

"Marie! Jeanne! Louis!" he cried in a voice of love. "Don't you know me after all these weary months of prison and barrel? How I have searched for you!"

Immediately his family clustered around him with embraces and kisses.

"But, Father, how did you find us here?" cried little Louis at last.

"A ragged lad I met on the highway told me where you live," answered the knight.

"The Christ child," said Marie reverently, and told him the story.

And so, forever after, they and all their descendants have burned a candle in the window on the eve of Noel to light the solitary Christ child on his way.

THE CHRISTMAS TREE

MARY AUSTIN

When Mathew, for so the boy was called, was ten years old, he began to be of use about the charcoal pits, to mark the trees for cutting, to sack the coals, to keep the house, and to cook his father's meals. He had no companions of his own age nor wanted any, for at this time he loved the silver firs. A group of them grew in a swale below the cabin, tall and fine; the earth under them was slippery and brown with needles. Around them stood a ring of saplings and seedlings scattered there by the parent firs, and a little apart from these was the one that Mathew loved. It was slender of trunk and silvery white, the branches spread out fanwise to the outline of a perfect spire. Then he garlanded it with flowers and hung streamers of white clematis all heavy with bloom upon its boughs. He brought it berries in cups of bark and sweet water from the spring; always as long as he knew it, it seemed to him that the fir tree had a soul.

Mathew told it all his thoughts. When at times there was a heaviness in his breast which was really a longing for his mother, though he did not understand it, he would part the low spreading branches and creep up to the slender trunk of the fir. Then he would put his arms around it and be quiet for a long, beautiful time. The tree had its own way of comforting him; the branches swept the ground and shut him in dark and close. He made a little cairn of stones under it and kept his treasures there.

Often as he sat snuggled up to the heart of the tree, the boy would slip his hand over the smooth intervals between the whorls of boughs, and wonder how they knew the way to grow. Mathew noticed and pondered the secret of the silver fir and grew up with it until he was twelve years old and tall and strong for his age. By this time the charcoal burner began to be troubled about the boy's schooling.

Meantime there was rioting and noise and coming and going of strangers in the town at the foot of Pine Mountain, and the furnace blast went on ruddily and smokily. Because of the things he heard, Mathew was afraid; and on rare occasions when he went down to it, he sat quietly among the charcoal sacks, and would not go far away from them except when he held his father by the hand. After a time it seemed life went more quietly there, flowers began to grow in the yards of the houses, and children walked in the streets with books upon their arms.

"Where are they going, Father?" said the boy.

"To school," said the charcoal burner.

"And may I go?" asked Mathew.

"Not yet, my son."

But one day his father pointed out the foundations of a new building going up in the town.

"It is a church," he said, "and when that is finished it will be a sign that there will be women here like your mother; and then you may go to school."

Mathew ran and told the fir tree all about it.

"But I will never forget you, never," he cried, and he kissed the trunk. Day by day, from the spur of the mountain, he watched the church building; and it was wonderful how much he could see in that clear, thin atmosphere. No other building in town interested him so much. He saw the walls go up and the roof, and the spire rise skyward with something that glittered twinkling on its top. Then they painted the church white and hung a bell in the tower. Mathew fancied he could hear it on Sundays as he saw the people moving along like specks in the streets.

"Next week," said the father, "school begins, and it is time for you to go as I promised. I will come to see you once a month; and when the term is over, you shall come back to the mountain."

Mathew said goodbye to the fir tree, and there were tears in his eyes though he was happy. "I shall think of you very often," he said, "and wonder how you are getting along."

There were so many people in the town that it was quite as strange and fearful to him as it would be to you who have grown up in town to be left alone in the wood. At night, when he saw the charcoal burner's fires glowing up in the air where the bulk of the mountain melted into the dark, he would cry a little under the blankets; but after he began to learn, there was no more occasion for crying. It was to the child as though there had been a candle lighted in a dark room. On Sunday he went to the church, and then it was both light and music; for he heard the minister read about God in the Great Book and believed it all, for everything that happens in the wood is true and people who grow up in it are best at believing. Mathew thought it was all as the minister said, that there is nothing better than pleasing God. Then when he lay awake at night, he would try to think how it would have been with him if he had never come to this place. In his heart he began to be afraid of the time when he would have to go back to the mountain, where there was no one to tell him about this most important thing in the world, for his father never talked to him of these things. It preyed upon his mind; but if anyone noticed it, they thought that he pined for his father and wished himself at home.

It drew toward midwinter, and the white cap on The Hill of Summer Snow, which never quite melted even in the warmest weather, began to spread downward until it reached the charcoal burner's home. There was a great stir and excitement among the children, for it had been decided to have a Christmas tree in the church. Every Sunday now the Christ-child story was told over and grew near and brighter like the Christmas star. Mathew had not known about it before, except that on a certain day in the year his

father had bought him toys. He had supposed that it was because it was stormy and he had to be indoors. Now he was wrapped up in the story of love and sacrifice and felt his heart grow larger as he breathed it in, looking upon clear windless nights to see if he might discern the Star of Bethlehem rising over Pine Mountain and the Christ child come walking on the snow. It was not that he really expected it, but that the story was so alive in him. Mathew wished in his heart that he might never go away from this place. He sat in his seat in church, and all that the minister said sank deeply into his mind.

When it came time to decide about the tree, because Mathew's father was a charcoal burner and knew where the best trees grew, it was quite natural to ask him to furnish the tree for his part. Mathew fairly glowed with delight, and his father was pleased, too, for he liked to have his son noticed. The Saturday before Christmas was the time set for going for the tree, and by that time Mathew had quite settled in his mind that it should be his silver fir. He did not know how otherwise he could bring the tree to share in his new delight, nor what else he had worth giving, for he quite believed what he had been told, that it is only through giving the best beloved that one comes to the heart's desire. With all his heart Mathew wished never to live in any place where he might not hear about God. So when his father was ready with the ropes and the sharpened axe, the boy led the way to the silver firs.

"Why, that is a little beauty," said the charcoal burner, "and just the right size."

They were obliged to shovel away the snow to get at it for cutting, and Mathew turned away his face when the chips began to fly. The tree fell upon its side with a shuddering sigh; little beads of clear resin stood out about the scar of the axe. It seemed as if the tree wept. But how graceful and trim it looked when it stood in the church waiting for gifts! Mathew hoped that it would understand.

The charcoal burner came to church on Christmas Eve, the first time in many years. It makes a difference about these things when you have a son to take part in them. The church and the tree were alight with candles; to the boy it seemed like what he supposed the place of dreams might be. One large candle burned on the top of the tree and threw out pointed rays like a star; it made the charcoal burner's son think of Bethlehem. Then he heard the minister talking, and it was all of a cross and a star; but Mathew could only look at the tree and he felt that he had betrayed it. Then the choir began to sing, and the candle on top of the tree burned down quite low, and Mathew saw the slender cross of the topmost bough stand up dark before it. Suddenly he remembered his old puzzle: how the smallest twigs were divided off, each in the shape of a cross; how the boughs repeated the star form every year; and what was true of his fir was true of them all. Then it must have been that there were tears in his eyes, for he could not see plainly: the pillars of the church spread upward like the shafts of the trees and the organ playing was like the sound of the wind in their branches and the stately star-built firs rose up like spires, taller than the church tower, each with a cross on top. The sapling which was still before him trembled more, moving its boughs as

if it spoke; and the boy heard it in his heart and believed, for it spoke to him of God. Then all the fear went out of his heart and he had no more dread of going back to the mountain to spend his days, for now he knew that he need never be away from the green reminder of hope and sacrifice in the star and the cross of the silver fir; and the thought broadened in his mind that he might find more in the forest than he had ever thought to find, now that he knew what to look for, since everything speaks of God in its own way—it is only a matter of understanding.

It was very gay in the little church that Christmas night, with laughter and bonbons flying about, and every child had a package of candy and an armful of gifts. The charcoal burner had his pockets bulging full of toys, and Mathew's eyes glowed like the banked fires of the charcoal pits as they walked home in the keen, windless night.

"Well, my boy," said the charcoal burner, "I am afraid you will not be wanting to go back to the mountain with me after this."

"Oh, yes, I will," said Mathew happily, "for I think the mountains know quite as much of the important things as they know here in the town."

"Right you are," said the charcoal burner, as he clapped his boy's hand between both his own, "and I am pleased to think you have turned out such a sensible little fellow." But he really did not know all that was in his son's heart.

BEHIND THE WHITE BRICK

FRANCES HODGSON BURNETT

*J*em knew what to expect when Aunt Hetty began a day by calling her "Jemima." It was one of the poor child's grievances that she had been given such an ugly name. In all the books she had read, and she had read a great many, Jem never had met a heroine who was called Jemima. But it had been her mother's favorite sister's name, and so it had fallen to her lot. Her mother always called her "Jem," or "Mimi," which was much prettier, and even Aunt Hetty only reserved Jemima for unpleasant state occasions.

It was a dreadful day to Jem. Her mother was not at home, and would not be until night. She had been called away unexpectedly, and had been obliged to leave Jem and the baby to Aunt Hetty's mercies.

So Jem found herself busy enough. Scarcely had she finished doing one thing, when Aunt Hetty told her to begin another. She wiped dishes and picked fruit and attended to the baby; and when Baby had gone to sleep and everything else seemed disposed of, for a time, at least, she was so tired that she was glad to sit down.

And then she thought of the book she had been reading the night before—a certain delightful storybook about a little girl whose name was Flora who was so happy and rich and pretty and good that Jem had likened her to the little princesses one reads about.

"I shall have time to finish my chapter before dinnertime comes," said Jem, and she sat down snugly in one corner of the wide, old-fashioned fireplace.

But she had not read more than two pages before something dreadful happened. Aunt Hetty came into the room in a great hurry—in such a hurry, indeed, that she caught her foot in the matting and fell, striking her elbow sharply against a chair, which so upset her temper that the moment she found herself on her feet she flew at Jem.

"What!" she said, snatching the book from her. "Reading again, when I am running all over the house for you?" And she flung the pretty little blue-covered volume into the fire.

Jem sprang to rescue it with a cry, but it was impossible to reach it; it had fallen into a great hollow of red coal, and the blaze caught it at once.

"You are a wicked woman!" cried Jem, in a dreadful passion, to Aunt Hetty. "You are a very wicked woman."

Then matters reached a climax. Aunt Hetty boxed her ears, pushed her back on her

little footstool, and walked out of the room.

Jem hid her face on her arms and cried as if her heart would break. She cried until her eyes were heavy; but just as she was thinking of going to sleep, something fell down the chimney and made her look up. It was a piece of mortar, and she bent forward and looked up to see where it had come from. The chimney was so very wide that this was easy enough. She could see where the mortar had fallen from the side and left a white patch.

"How white it looks against the black," said Jem, "it is like a white brick among the black ones. What queer place a chimney is!"

And then a funny thought came into her fanciful little head. How many things were burned in the big fireplace and vanished in smoke or tinder up the chimney! Where did everything go? There was Flora, for instance, Where was she by this time? Certainly there was nothing left of her in the fire. Jem almost began to cry again at the thought.

"It was too bad," she said. "She was so pretty and funny and I did like her so."

I dare say it scarcely will be credited by unbelieving people when I tell them what happened next. Jem felt herself gradually lifted off her little footstool.

"Oh!" she said, timidly, "how very light I feel! Oh, dear, I'm going up the chimney. I've heard Aunt Hetty talk about the draft drawing things up the chimney, but I never knew it was as strong as this."

She went up, up, up, quietly and steadily, and without any uncomfortable feeling at all; and then all at once she stopped, feeling that her feet rested against something solid. She opened her eyes and looked about her, and there she was, standing right opposite the white brick, her feet on a tiny ledge.

"Well," she said, "this is funny."

But the next thing that happened was funnier still. She found that, without thinking what she was doing, she was knocking on the white brick with her knuckles, as if it were a door and she expected somebody to open it. The next minute she heard footsteps, and then a sound, as if someone were drawing back a little bolt.

"It is a door," said Jem, "and somebody is going to open it."

The white brick moved a little, and some more mortar and soot fell; then the brick moved a little more, and then it slid aside and left an open space.

"It's a room!" cried Jem, "There's a room behind it!"

And so there was, and before the open space stood a pretty little girl with long lovely hair and a fringe on her forehead. Jem clasped her hands in amazement. It was Flora herself, as she looked in the picture.

"Come in," she said. "I thought it was you."

"But how can I come in through such a little place?" asked Jem.

"Oh, that is easy enough," said Flora. "Here, give me your hand."

Jem did as she told her, and found that it was easy enough. In an instant she had passed through the opening, the white brick had gone back to its place, and she was standing by Flora's side in a large room—the nicest room she had ever seen. It was big and lofty and light, and

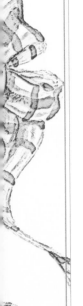

there were all kinds of delightful things in it—books and flowers and playthings and pictures and, in one corner, a great cage full of lovebirds.

"Have I ever seen it before?" asked Jem, glancing slowly round.

"Why," said Flora, laughing, "it's my room, the one you read about last night."

She led the way out of the room and down a little passage with several doors on each side, and she opened one door and showed Jem what was on the other side. That was a room, too, and this time it was funny as well as pretty. Both floor and walls were padded with rose color, and the floor was strewn with toys. There were big soft balls, rattles, horses, woolly dogs, and a doll or so; there was one low cushioned chair and a low table.

"You can come in," said a shrill little voice behind the door, "only mind you don't tread on things."

"What a funny little voice!" said Jem, but she had no sooner said it than she jumped back.

The owner of the voice, who had just come forward, was no other than Baby.

"Why," exclaimed Jem, beginning to feel frightened, "I left you fast asleep in your crib."

"Did you?" said Baby, somewhat scornfully. "That's just the way with you grown-up people. You think you know everything, and yet you haven't discretion enough to know when a pin is sticking into one. You'd know soon enough if you had one sticking into your own back."

"But I'm not grown up," stammered Jem. "And when you are at home you can neither walk nor talk. You're not six months old."

"Well, Miss," retorted Baby, whose wrongs seemed to have soured her disposition some-what, "you have no need to throw that in my teeth; you were not six months old, either, when you were my age."

Jem could not help laughing. "You haven't got any teeth," she said.

"Haven't I?" said Baby, and she displayed two beautiful rows with some haughtiness of manner. "When I am up here," she said, "I am supplied with the modern conveniences, and that's why I never complain. Do I ever cry when I am asleep? It's not falling asleep I object to, it's falling awake."

"Wait a minute," said Jem. "Are you asleep now?"

"I'm what you call asleep. I can only come here when I'm what you call asleep. Asleep, indeed! It's no wonder we always cry when we have to fall awake."

"I suppose you would like me to show you round?" she said.

"Not if you have any objection," replied Jem, who was rather subdued.

"I would as soon do it as not," said Baby. She stopped at the first door she came to and knocked three times. She was obliged to stand upon tiptoe to reach the knocker.

"He's sure to be at home at this time of year," she remarked. "This is the busy season."

"Who's 'he'?" inquired Jem.

But Flora only laughed at Miss Baby's consequential air.

"S. C., to be sure," was the answer, as the young lady pointed to the doorplate, upon which Jem noticed, for the first time, "S. C." in very large letters.

The door opened, apparently without

assistance, and they entered the apartment.

"Good gracious!" exclaimed Jem, the next minute. "Goodness gracious!"

She might well be astonished. It was such a long room that she could not see to the end of it; and it was piled up from floor to ceiling with toys of every description; and there was such bustle and buzzing in it that it was quite confusing. The bustle and buzzing in it arose from a very curious cause too. It was the bustle and buzz of hundreds of tiny men and women who were working at little tables no higher than mushrooms—the pretty, tiny women cutting out and sewing, the pretty, tiny men sawing and hammering, and all talking at once. The principal person in the place escaped Jem's notice at first; but it was not long before she saw him, a little, old gentleman, with a rosy face and sparkling eyes, sitting at a desk and writing in a book almost as big as himself. He was so busy that he was quite excited and had been obliged to throw his white fur coat and cap aside, and he was at work in his red waistcoat.

"Look here, if you please," piped Baby. "I have brought someone to see you."

When he turned round, Jem recognized him.

"Eh! Eh!" he said. "What! What! Who's this, Tootsicums?"

Baby's manner became very acid indeed.

"I shouldn't have thought you would have said that, Mr. Santa Claus," she remarked. "I can't help myself down below, but I generally have my rights respected up here."

"Come, come!" said S. C. chuckling comfortably and rubbing his hands. "Don't be too dignified—it's a bad thing. And don't be too fond of flourishing your rights in people's faces—that's the worst of all, Miss Midget. Folks who make such a fuss about their rights turn them into wrongs sometimes."

Then he turned suddenly to Jem. "You are the little girl from down below," he said.

"Yes, sir," answered Jem. "I'm Jem, and this is my friend Flora—out of the blue book."

"I'm happy to make her acquaintance," said S. C., "and I'm happy to make yours. You are a nice child, though a trifle peppery. I'm very glad to see you."

"I'm very glad indeed to see you, sir," said Jem. "I wasn't quite sure—"

But there she stopped, feeling that it would be scarcely polite to tell him that she had begun of late years to lose faith in him.

But S. C. only chuckled more comfortably than ever and rubbed his hands again.

"Ho, ho!" he said. "You know who I am, then?"

Jem hesitated a moment, wondering whether it would not be taking a liberty to mention his name without putting "Mr." before it; then she remembered what Baby had called him.

"Baby called you 'Mr. Claus,' sir," she replied, "and I have seen pictures of you."

"To be sure," said S. C. "S. Claus, Esquire, of Chimneyland. How do you like me?"

"Very much," answered Jem, "very much indeed, sir."

"Glad of it! Glad of it! But what was it you were going to say you were not quite sure of?"

Jem blushed a little.

"I was not quite sure of that—that you were true, sir. At least I have not been quite sure since I have been older."

S. C. rubbed the bald part of his head and gave a little sigh.

"I hope I have not hurt your feelings, sir," faltered Jem, who was a very kind-hearted soul.

"Well, no," said S. C. "Not exactly. And it is not your fault either. It is nature, I suppose; at any rate, it is the way of the world. People lose their belief in a great many things as they grow older; but that does not make the things not true, thank goodness! And their faith often comes back after a while. But bless me!" he added briskly, "Suppose I show you my establishment; come with me."

It really would be quite impossible to describe the wonderful things he showed them. Jem's head was quite in a whirl before she had seen one-half of them, and even Baby condescended to become excited.

"There must be a great many children in the world, Mr. Claus," ventured Jem.

"Yes, yes, millions of 'em; bless 'em," said S. C., growing rosier with delight at the very thought. "We never run out of them, that's one comfort. There's a large and varied assortment always on hand. Fresh ones every year, too; so that when one grows too old, there is a new one ready. I have a place like this in every twelfth chimney."

S. C. showed them the rest of his wonders, and then went with them to the door to bid them goodbye.

"I am sure we are very much obliged to you, Mr. Claus," said Jem, gratefully. "I shall never again think you are not true, sir."

S. C. patted her shoulder quite affectionately.

"That's right," he said. "Believe in things just as long as you can, my dear. Goodbye until Christmas Eve. I shall see you this year, if you don't see me."

"How kind he is!" exclaimed Jem.

And then, suddenly, a very strange feeling came over Jem. Without being able to account for it at all, she found herself still sitting on her little stool, with a beautiful scarlet and gold book at her knee and her mother standing by laughing at her amazed face. As for Miss Baby, she was crying as hard as she could in her crib.

"Mother!" Jem cried, "have you really come home as early as this, and," rubbing her eyes in great amazement, "how did I come down?"

"Don't I look as if I were real?" said her mother, laughing and kissing her. "And doesn't your present look real? I don't know how you came down, I'm sure. Where have you been?"

Jem shook her head very mysteriously. She saw that her mother fancied she had been asleep, but she herself knew better.

"I know you wouldn't believe it were true if I told you," she said. "I have been *behind the white brick*."

CHANGED BY CHRISTMAS

A CHRISTMAS CAROL

CHARLES DICKENS

Old Scrooge was a tight-fisted man, he was! Why, old Jacob Marley had been dead for seven years, yet Scrooge had not even had Marley's name painted out over the door to the counting house. . . .

Now once upon a time on a cold and groggy Christmas Eve, Scrooge sat counting his money in his counting house. The door to his office was open so he could keep an eye on his clerk, Bob Cratchit. Poor Bob was wrapped in a long woolen muffler because Scrooge was too stingy to allow him a fire.

With a sudden gust of wind, the door flew open as Scrooge's nephew stepped in to wish his uncle a "Merry Christmas." The only reply from Scrooge was a harsh "Bah humbug!" Moments after his nephew's departure, the door was pushed open again, and two gentlemen entered.

"Good day, kind sir," said one. "We are raising funds for the poor this Christmas season. What shall I put you down for?"

"Nothing!" replied Scrooge. "It is no concern of mine if these folks are poor."

The two men shook their heads at his angry words and turned to leave.

Scrooge turned to look at his clerk. "I suppose you want all day tomorrow off. You may have it," he said grudgingly, "but you had better be in early the next day." And with that, Scrooge stomped out the door and headed home.

As Scrooge began to turn the key in his door, he noticed something strange about the big brass knocker on the door. From the center of it glowed a ghostly face, with spectacles upon its forehead. Why, it looked as his old partner, Marley, used to look!

Scrooge's spine tingled and the hair stood up on the back of his neck. As he stared at the ghostly face, it became a knocker again. He dashed into the house and up into his room where he locked the door twice.

As Scrooge sat alone sipping a small bowl of gruel, his mind returned to the knocker. "Humbug!" he said to himself.

No sooner had he said this than strange noises began to sound. And right through the twice-locked door, a ghost appeared—a ghost dressed in Marley's coat and boots, but also wrapped in chains made of keys, cashboxes, and bankbooks!

"Who are you?" Scrooge whispered. "What do you want?"

"Much," said the ghost of Marley. "I lived a wasted and selfish life—caring only about money—and now I must wander like this forever, weighed down by these chains. But you, Ebenezer, have yet a chance to escape my fate.

"You will be haunted," the ghost continued, "by three spirits. Expect the first tomorrow when the clock strikes one. You will see me no more, but remember what I have said."

And with that, the ghost of Jacob Marley slipped out the window into the foggy night air. And Scrooge turned and went straight to bed.

When Scrooge awoke, he heard the clock strike one in the stillness of the night. Suddenly a strange figure stood beside his bed. It had long white hair, but a smooth, fair face without a wrinkle. And from its head, a beam of light glowed.

Scrooge clutched his blankets to his chin and asked, "Are you the spirit whose coming was foretold to me?"

"Yes," it said. "I am the Spirit of Christmas Past. Rise and walk with me."

They were instantly transported to the office where Scrooge had worked as a young man.

"Why, it's Old Fezziwig!" exclaimed Scrooge.

As he watched, his old boss slapped a younger Scrooge on the back and said, "No more work tonight, it's Christmas Eve. Let's clear the floor and set up for a party."

Watching this delightful scene, Scrooge thought back to yet another Christmas past. He sat beside a young girl whose eyes were filled with tears.

"I cannot marry you, Ebenezer," she said softly, "for you love your money more than I." A single tear ran down her cheek, then she turned and left.

"Spirit," Scrooge cried. "Show me no more. Take me home."

"Come then," the spirit answered. "My time is short. We must return."

Immediately Scrooge was back in his own room, on his bed in a heavy sleep.

Awaking in the middle of a snore, Scrooge again heard the clock strike one. Looking around, he saw his room; and yet something was strange. The room was not as he remembered. The walls were hung with holly, and a roaring fire filled the room with light, and heaped on the floor was a steaming, fragrant feast.

Seated amidst this feast was an enormous, laughing giant. "Come in," he boomed. "I am the Spirit of Christmas Present."

He reached his hand toward Scrooge and commanded, "Touch my robe."

Instantly they were transported through the snowy streets to the house of poor Bob Cratchit. It was a simple house, yet filled with life and love.

Tiny Tim, a small, pale child who carried a crutch, sat close to his father. As the Christmas meal drew to a close, Bob raised his cup and said, "A Merry Christmas to us all. God bless us."

"God bless us every one!" cried Tiny Tim.

Bob held his son's small hand in his own, for he loved the child and feared Tiny Tim would not live to see another Christmas.

"Spirit," said Scrooge. "Tell me if Tiny Tim will live."

"I see an empty chair," replied the spirit. "If these shadows remain unchanged by the

future, then the child will die."

The clock struck again; the spirit disappeared. Frightened, Scrooge peered into the darkness around him. He saw a dark and frightening shape moving toward him. Beneath the shadowy hood of the spirit's robe, two ghostly eyes pierced him with an icy stare.

"Are you the Ghost of Christmas Yet to Come?" he asked.

The spirit nodded slightly and began to move ahead. Scrooge followed to the home of Bob Cratchit, where they noticed Tiny Tim's empty chair in a corner.

Then the spirit carried Scrooge away to an old weed-choked churchyard. In the deeply carved granite of one of the stones, his name could be read: EBENEZER SCROOGE.

He shrieked, "Oh, hear me, Spirit! Tell me I have hope of changing what you have shown me. I will honor Christmas in my heart and try to keep it all year. Help me change the future as I saw it here!"

He caught the spirit's hand; but as he did so, it changed into a bedpost—his bedpost.

"I will live in the past, the present, and the future," Scrooge cried joyfully as he climbed out of bed. "Oh, thank you, Jacob Marley. Thank you most sincerely!"

And Ebenezer Scrooge was better than his word. He did it all and even more; and to Tiny Tim, who did not die, he was a second father. He became as good a friend, master, and man as anyone ever knew. From that day on, it was always said that Ebenezer Scrooge knew how to keep Christmas well.

May that be said of each of us. And so, as Tiny Tim observed: God bless us every one!

THE LITTLE MATCH-SELLER

HANS CHRISTIAN ANDERSEN

It was terribly cold and nearly dark on the last evening of the old year, and the snow was falling fast. In the cold and the darkness, a poor little girl, with bare head and naked feet, roamed through the streets. It is true she had on a pair of slippers when she left home, but they were not of much use. They were very large, so large that they had belonged to her mother, and the poor little creature had lost them in running across the street to avoid two carriages that were rolling along at a terrible rate. One of the slippers she could not find, and a boy seized upon the other and ran away with it, saying that he could use it as a cradle, when he had children of his own. So the little girl went on with her little naked feet, which were quite red and blue with the cold. In an old apron she carried a number of matches, and had a bundle of them in her hands. No one had bought anything of her the whole day, nor had anyone given her even a penny. Shivering with cold and hunger, she crept along; poor little child, she looked the picture of misery. The snowflakes fell on her long, fair hair, which hung in curls on her shoulders, but she regarded them not.

Lights were shining from every window, and there was a savory smell of roast goose, for it was Christmas Eve—yes, she remembered that. In a corner, between two houses, one of which projected beyond the other, she sank down and huddled herself together. She had drawn her little feet under her, but she could not keep off the cold; and she dared not go home, for she had sold no matches, and could not take home even a penny of money. Her father would certainly beat her; besides, it was almost as cold at home as here, for they had only the roof to cover them, through which the wind howled, although the largest holes had been stopped up with straw and rags. Her little hands were almost frozen with the cold. Ah! perhaps a burning match might be some good, if she could draw it from the bundle and strike it against the wall, just to warm her fingers. She drew one out—*scratch!*—how it sputtered as it burned! It gave a warm, bright light, like a little candle, as she held her hand over it. It was really a wonderful light. It seemed to the little girl that she was sitting by a large iron stove, with polished brass feet and a brass ornament. How the fire burned! It seemed so beautifully warm that the child stretched out her feet as if to warm them, when, lo! the flame of the match went out, the stove vanished, and she had only the remains of the half-burnt match in her hand.

She rubbed another match on the wall. It burst into a flame, and where its light fell

upon the wall it became as transparent as a veil, and she could see into the room. The table was covered with a snowy white tablecloth, on which stood a splendid dinner service, and a steaming roast goose, stuffed with apples and dried plums. And what was still more wonderful, the goose jumped down from the dish and waddled across the floor, with a knife and fork in its breast, to the little girl. Then the match went out, and there remained nothing but the thick, damp, cold wall before her.

She lighted another match, and then she found herself sitting under a beautiful Christmas tree. It was larger and more beautifully decorated than the one which she had seen through the glass door at the rich merchant's. Thousands of tapers were burning upon the green branches; and colored pictures, like those she had seen in the show-windows, looked down upon it all. The little one stretched out her hand toward them, and the match went out.

The Christmas lights rose higher and higher, till they looked to her like the stars in the sky. Then she saw a star fall, leaving behind it a bright streak of fire. "Someone is dying," thought the little girl, for her old grandmother, the only one who had ever loved her, and who was now dead, had told her that when a star falls, a soul is going up to God.

She again rubbed a match on the wall, and the light shone round her; in the brightness stood her old grandmother, clear and shining, yet mild and loving in her appearance.

"Grandmother," cried the little one, "oh, take me with you; I know you will go away when the match burns out; you will vanish like the warm stove, the roast goose, and the large, glorious Christmas tree."

And she made haste to light the whole bundle of matches, for she wished to keep her grandmother there. And the matches glowed with a light that was brighter than the noonday, and her grandmother had never appeared so large or so beautiful. She took the little girl in her arms, and they both flew upward in brightness and joy far above the earth, where there was neither cold nor hunger nor pain, for they were with God.

In the dawn of morning there lay the poor little one, with pale cheeks and smiling mouth, leaning against the wall. The child still sat, in the stiffness of death, holding the matches in her hand, one bundle of which was burnt. "She tried to warm herself," said some. No one imagined what beautiful things she had seen, nor into what glory she had entered with her grandmother, on Christmas Day.

CELEBRATING THE MIRACLES OF CHRISTMAS

❖ THE POWER OF CHRISTMAS TO CHANGE ❖

The Son of God, th' eternal King,
That did us all salvation bring,
And freed the soul from danger,
He whom the whole world could not take,
The Word, which Heaven and Earth did make,
Was now laid in a manger.

—BEN JONSON

Hard thoughts are
heavy to carry, my
friend, and life is short
from beginning to end;
be kind to yourself,
leave nothing to mend
when Christmas comes.

—WILLIAM LYTLE

Rise, happy morn; rise, holy morn;
Draw forth the cheerful day from night:
O Father, touch the east, and light the light
That shone when Hope was born.

—ALFRED, LORD TENNYSON

But peaceful was the night
Wherein the Prince of light
His reign of peace
Upon the earth began.

—JOHN MILTON

Oh, how joyfully, oh, how merrily,
Christmas comes with its grace divine!
Grace again is beaming;
Christ, the world redeeming:
Hail, ye Christians,
Hail the joyous Christmastime!

—J. FALK

Oh, how joyfully, oh, how merrily,

O Holy Night! The stars are brightly shining;
It is the night of the dear Savior's birth.
Long lay the world in sin and error pining,
Till He appeared and the spirit felt its worth.
A thrill of hope, the weary world rejoices,
For yonder breaks a new and glorious morn.

—Adolphe Adam

Somehow, not only for Christmas
But all the year through,
The joy that you give to others
Is the joy that comes back to you;
And the more you spend in blessing
The poor and lonely and sad,
The more of your heart's possessing
Returns to make you glad.

—John Greenleaf Whittier

Though I speak with the
tongues of men and of angels,
and have not charity, I am
become as sounding brass, or a
tinkling cymbal. . . . And now
abideth faith, hope, charity,
these three; but the greatest of
these is charity.

1 Corinthians 13:1,13

The earth has grown cold with its burden of care,
But at Christmas it always is young.
The heart of the jewel burns lustrous and fair,
And its soul full of music breaks forth on the air,
When the song of the angels is sung.

The feet of the humblest may walk in the field
Where the feet of the holiest have trod;
This, this is the marvel to mortals revealed,
When the silvery trumpets of Christmas have pealed,
That mankind are the children of God.

—Phillips Brooks

Christmas comes with its grace divine!

THE FIR TREE

HANS CHRISTIAN ANDERSEN

Far down in the forest, where the warm sun and the fresh air made a sweet resting place, grew a pretty little fir tree; and yet it was not happy. It wished so much to be tall like its companions—the pines and firs which grew around it. The sun shone, and the soft air fluttered its leaves, and the little peasant children passed by, prattling merrily, but the fir tree heeded them not.

Sometimes the children would bring a large basket of raspberries or strawberries, wreathed on a straw, and seat themselves near the fir tree, and say, "Is it not a pretty little tree?" which made it feel more unhappy than before. And yet all this while the tree grew a notch or joint taller every year; for by the number of joints in the stem of a fir tree we can discover its age.

Still, as it grew, it complained, "Oh, how I wish I were as tall as the other trees, then I would spread out my branches on every side, and my top would overlook the wide world. I should have the birds building their nests on my boughs, and when the wind blew, I should bow with stately dignity like my tall companions." The tree was so discontented that it took no pleasure in the warm sunshine, the birds, or the rosy clouds that floated over it morning and evening.

Sometimes, in winter, when the snow lay white and glittering on the ground, a hare would come springing along and jump right over the little tree; and then how mortified it would feel! Two winters passed, and when the third arrived, the tree had grown so tall that the hare was obliged to run round it. Yet it remained unsatisfied, and would exclaim, "Oh, if I could but keep on growing tall and old! There is nothing else worth caring for in the world!"

In the autumn, as usual, the woodcutters came and cut down several of the tallest trees, and the young fir tree, which was now grown to its full height, shuddered as the noble trees fell to the earth with a crash. After the branches were lopped off, the trunks looked so slender and bare that they could scarcely be recognized. Then they were placed upon wagons, and drawn by horses out of the forest. Where were they going? What would become of them? The young fir tree wished very much to know; so in the spring, when the swallows and the storks came, it asked, "Do you know where those trees were taken? Did you meet them?"

The swallows knew nothing, but the stork, after a little reflection, nodded his head, and said, "Yes, I think I do. I met several new ships when I flew from Egypt, and they had fine masts that smelled like fir. I think these must have been the trees; I assure you they were stately, very stately."

"Oh, how I wish I were tall enough to go on the sea," said the fir tree. "What is the sea, and what does it look like?"

"It would take too much time to explain," said the stork, flying away.

"Rejoice in thy youth," said the sunbeam; "rejoice in thy fresh growth, and the young life that is in thee."

And the wind kissed the tree, and the dew watered it; but the fir tree regarded them not.

Christmastime drew near; and many young trees were cut down, some even smaller and younger than the fir tree who enjoyed neither rest nor peace with longing to leave its forest home. These young trees, which were chosen for their beauty, kept their branches and were also laid on wagons and drawn by horses out of the forest.

"Where are they going?" asked the fir tree. "They are not taller than I am; indeed, one is much less. And why are the branches not cut off? Where are they going?"

"We know, we know," sang the sparrows; "we have looked in at the windows of the houses in the town, and we know what is done with them. They are dressed up in the most splendid manner. We have seen them standing in the middle of a warm room, and adorned with all sorts of beautiful things—honey cakes, gilded apples, playthings, and many hundreds of wax tapers."

"And," asked the fir tree, trembling through all its branches, "and then what happens?"

"We did not see any more," said the sparrows; "but this was enough for us."

"I wonder whether anything so brilliant will ever happen to me," thought the fir tree. "It would be much better than crossing the sea. I long for it almost with pain. When will Christmas be here? I am now as tall and well grown as those which were taken away last year. Oh, that I were now laid on the wagon, or standing in the warm room, with all that brightness and splendor around me! Something better and more beautiful is to come after, or the trees would not be so decked out. Yes, what follows will be grander and more splendid. What can it be? I am weary with longing. I scarcely know how I feel."

"Rejoice with us," said the air and the sunlight. "Enjoy thine own life in the fresh air."

But the tree would not rejoice, though it grew taller every day; and, winter and summer, its dark-green foliage might be seen in the forest, while passersby would say, "What a beautiful tree!"

A short time before Christmas, the discontented fir tree was the first to fall. As the axe cut through the stem and divided the pith, the tree fell with a groan to the earth, conscious of pain and faintness, and forgetting all its anticipations of happiness, in sorrow at leaving its home in the forest. It knew that it should never again see its dear old companions: the trees, nor the little bushes and many-colored flowers that had grown by its side, perhaps not even the birds. Neither was the journey at all pleasant. The tree first recovered itself while being unpacked in the courtyard of a house, with several other trees;

and it heard a man say, "We only want one, and this is the prettiest."

Then came two servants and carried the fir tree into a large and beautiful apartment. There were rocking chairs, silken sofas, large tables, covered with pictures, books, and playthings, worth a great deal of money—at least, the children said so. The fir tree was placed in a large tub, full of sand; and it stood on a very handsome carpet. How the fir tree trembled! What was going to happen to him now? Some young ladies came, and the servants helped them to adorn the tree. On one branch they hung little bags cut out of colored paper; from other branches hung gilded apples and walnuts; and above were hundreds of red, blue, and white tapers, which were fastened on the branches. Dolls, exactly like real babies, were placed under the green leaves and at the very top was fastened a glittering star, made of tinsel. Oh, it was very beautiful!

"This evening," they all exclaimed, "how bright it will be!"

"Oh, that the evening were come," thought the tree, "and the tapers lighted! Then I shall know what else is going to happen. Will the trees of the forest come to see me? I wonder if the sparrows will peep in at the windows as they fly? Shall I grow faster here, and keep on all these ornaments summer and winter?"

But guessing was of very little use; it made his back ache, and this pain is as bad for a slender fir tree as a headache is for us. At last the tapers were lighted, and then what a glistening blaze of light the tree presented! It trembled so with joy in all its branches, that one of the candles fell among the green leaves and burnt some of them.

After this, the tree tried not to tremble at all, though the fire frightened him; he was so anxious not to hurt any of the beautiful ornaments, even while their brilliancy dazzled him. And now the folding doors were thrown open, and a troop of children rushed in as if they intended to upset the tree; they were followed more silently by their elders. For a moment the little ones stood silent with astonishment, and then they shouted for joy, till the room rang, and they danced merrily round the tree, while one present after another was taken from it.

"What are they doing? What will happen next?" thought the fir. At last the candles burnt down to the branches and were put out. Then the children received permission to plunder the tree.

Oh, how they rushed upon it, till the branches cracked, and had it not been fastened with the glistening star to the ceiling, it would have been thrown down. The children then danced about with their pretty toys, and no one noticed the tree, except the children's maid who came and peeped among the branches to see if an apple or a fig had been forgotten.

"A story, a story," cried the children, pulling a little fat man towards the tree.

"Now we shall be in the green shade," said the man, as he seated himself under it, "and the tree will have the pleasure of hearing also, but I shall only relate one story; what shall it be? Ivede-Avede, or Humpty Dumpty, who fell down stairs, but soon got up again, and at last married a princess."

"Ah! yes, so it happens in the world,"

upstairs to the garret, and threw him on the floor, in a dark corner, where no daylight shone, and there they left him.

"What does this mean?" thought the tree. "What am I to do here? I can hear nothing in a place like this." "It is winter now," thought the tree, "the ground is hard and covered with snow, so that people cannot plant me. I shall be sheltered here, I dare say, until spring comes. How pleasant it was out in the forest while the snow lay on the ground, when the hare would run by, yes, and jump over me, too, although I did not like it then. Oh, it is terribly lonely here."

"Squeak, squeak," said a little mouse, creeping cautiously towards the tree; then came another; and they both sniffed at the fir tree and crept between the branches.

"Oh, it is very cold," said the little mouse, "or else we should be so comfortable here, shouldn't we, you old fir tree?"

"I am not old," said the fir tree, "there are many who are older than I am."

"Where do you come from? And what do you know?" asked the mice, who were full of curiosity. And then the tree told the little mice all about its youth. They had never heard such an account in their lives; and after they had listened to it attentively, they said, "What a number of things you have seen! You must have been very happy."

"Happy!" exclaimed the fir tree; and then as he reflected upon what he had been telling them, he said, "Ah, yes! after all those were happy days." But when he went on and related all about Christmas Eve, and how he had been dressed up with cakes and lights, the mice said, "How happy

thought the fir tree; he believed it all, because it was related by such a nice man. "Ah! well," he thought, "who knows? Perhaps I may fall down too, and marry a princess"; and he looked forward joyfully to the next evening, expecting to be again decked out with lights and playthings, gold and fruit. "Tomorrow I will not tremble," thought he; "I will enjoy all my splendor, and I shall hear the story of Humpty Dumpty again, and perhaps Ivede-Avede."

And the tree remained quiet and thoughtful all night. In the morning the servants and the housemaid came in. "Now," thought the fir, "all my splendor is going to begin again." But they dragged him out of the room and you must have been, you old fir tree."

"I am not old at all," replied the tree, "I only came from the forest this winter; I am now checked in my growth."

"What splendid stories you can relate," said the little mice. And the next night four other mice came with them to hear what the tree had to tell. The more he talked the more he remembered, and then he thought to himself, "Those were happy days, but they may come again."

"Who is Humpty Dumpty?" asked the little mice. And then the tree related the whole story; he could remember every single word, and the little mice were so delighted with it that they were ready to jump to the top of the tree. The next night a great many more mice made their appearance, and on Sunday two rats came with them; but they said, it was not a pretty story at all, and the little mice were very sorry, for it made them also think less of it.

"Do you know only one story?" asked the rats.

"Only one," replied the fir tree; "I heard it on the happiest evening of my life; but I did not know I was so happy at the time."

"Many thanks to you then," replied the rats, and they marched off.

The little mice also kept away after this, and the tree sighed, and said, "It was very pleasant when the merry little mice sat round me and listened while I talked. Now that is all past too. However, I shall consider myself happy when someone comes to take me out of this place."

But would this ever happen? Yes; one morning people came to clear out the garret, the boxes were packed away, and the tree was pulled out of the corner, and thrown roughly on the garret floor; then the servant dragged it out upon the staircase where the daylight shone.

"Now life is beginning again," said the tree, rejoicing in the sunshine and fresh air. Then it was carried down stairs and taken into the court-yard so quickly that it forgot to think of itself, and could only look about, there was so much to be seen.

The court was close to a garden, where everything looked blooming. Fresh and fragrant roses hung over the little palings. The linden trees were in blossom; while the swallows flew here and there, crying, "Twit, twit, twit, my mate is coming," but it was not the fir tree they meant.

"Now I shall live," cried the tree, joyfully spreading out its branches; but alas! They were all withered and yellow and the tree lay in a corner among weeds and nettles. The star of gold paper still stuck in the top of the tree and glittered in the sunshine. In the same courtyard two of the merry children were playing who had danced round the tree at Christmas and had been so happy. The youngest saw the gilded star, and ran and pulled it off the tree.

"Look what is sticking to the ugly old fir tree," said the child, treading on the branches till they crackled under his boots. And the tree saw all the fresh, bright flowers in the garden, and then looked at itself, and wished it had remained in the dark corner of the garret. It thought of its fresh youth in the forest, of the merry Christmas evening, and of the little mice who had listened to the story of Humpty Dumpty.

"Past! Past!" said the old tree; "Oh, had I but enjoyed myself while I could have done so!

But now it is too late." Then a lad came and chopped the tree into small pieces, till a large bundle lay in a heap on the ground. The pieces were placed in a fire under the copper, and they quickly blazed up brightly, while the tree sighed so deeply that each sigh was like a pistol shot.

Then the children, who were at play, came and seated themselves in front of the fire, and looked at it and cried, "Pop, pop." But at each "pop," which was a deep sigh, the tree was thinking of a summer day in the forest; and of Christmas evening, and of "Humpty Dumpty," the only story it had ever heard or knew how to relate, till at last it was consumed. The boys still played in the garden, and the youngest wore the golden star on his breast, with which the tree had been adorned during the happiest evening of its existence. Now all was past; the tree's life was past, and the story also—for all stories must come to an end at last.

THE ELVES AND THE SHOEMAKER

THE BROTHERS GRIMM

Once upon a time there was a poor shoemaker. He made excellent shoes and worked quite diligently, but he could not earn enough to support himself and his family. He became so poor that he he could not even afford to buy the leather needed to make shoes. Finally he had only enough to make one last pair. He cut them out with great care and put the pieces on his workbench, so that he could sew them the following morning.

"Now I wonder," he sighed, "will I ever make another pair of shoes? Once I've sold this pair, I shall need all the money to buy food for my family. I will not be able to buy any new leather." That night, the shoemaker went to bed a sad and distraught man.

The next morning, he awoke and went down to his workshop. On his bench he found an exquisite pair of shoes! They had small and even stitches, formed so perfectly that he knew he couldn't have produced a better pair himself. Upon close examination, the shoes proved to be from the very pieces of leather he had set out the night before. He immediately put the fine pair of shoes in the window of his shop and drew back the blinds.

"Who in the world could've done this great service for me?" he asked himself. Even before he could make up an answer, a rich man strode into his shop and bought the shoes—and for a fancy price.

The shoemaker was ecstatic; he immediately went out and purchased plenty of food for his family and some more leather. That afternoon he cut out two pairs of shoes and, just as before, laid all the pieces on the bench so that he could sew them the next day. Then he went upstairs to enjoy the good meal with his family.

"My goodness!" he cried the next morning when he found two pairs of beautifully finished shoes on his workbench. "Who could make such fine shoes, and so quickly?" He put them in his shop window, and before long some wealthy people came in and paid a great deal of money for them. The shoemaker went right out and bought more leather.

For weeks, and then months, this continued. Whether the shoemaker cut two pairs or four pairs, the fine new shoes were always ready in the morning. Soon his small shop was crowded with customers. He cut out many types of shoes: stiff boots lined with fur, delicate slippers for dancers, walking shoes for ladies, tiny shoes for children. Soon his shoes had bows and laces and buckles of fine silver. The little shop prospered as never before, and its proprietor was soon a rich man himself. His family wanted for nothing.

As the shoemaker and his wife sat by the fire one night, he said, "One of these days, I shall have to learn who has been helping us."

"We could hide behind the cupboard in your workroom," she said. "That way, we could find out just who your helpers are." And that was just what they did.

That evening, when the clock struck twelve, the shoemaker and his wife heard a noise. Two tiny men, each with a bag of tools, were squeezing beneath a crack under the door.

The two men clambered onto the workbench and began working. Their little hands stitched and their little hammers tapped ceaselessly the whole night through.

"They are so small! And they make such beautiful shoes in no time at all!" the shoemaker whispered to his wife as the dawn rose.

"Quiet!" his wife answered. "See how they

A Jolly Xmas to you

are cleaning up now." And in an instant the two elves had disappeared beneath the door.

The next day, the shoemaker's wife said, "Those little elves have done so much good for us. Since it is nearly Christmas, we should make some gifts for them."

"Yes!" cried the shoemaker. "I'll make

some boots that will fit them, and you make some clothes." They worked until dawn. On Christmas Eve the presents were laid out upon the workbench: two tiny jackets, two pairs of trousers, and two little woolen caps. They also left out a plate of good things to eat and drink. Then they hid once again behind the cupboard and waited to see what would happen.

Just as before, the elves appeared at the stroke of midnight. They jumped onto the bench to begin their work, but when they saw all the presents they began to laugh and shout with joy. They tried on all the clothes, then helped themselves to the food and drink. Then they jumped down and danced excitedly around the workroom and disappeared beneath the door.

After Christmas, the shoemaker cut out his leather as he always had, but the two elves never returned. "I believe they have heard us whispering," his wife said. "Elves are so very shy when it comes to people, you know."

"I know I will miss their help," the shoemaker said, "but we will manage. The shop is always so busy now. But my stitches will never be as tight and small as theirs!"

The shoemaker did indeed continue to prosper, but he and his family always remembered the good elves who had helped them during the hard times. And each and every Christmas Eve from that year onward, they gathered around the fire to drink a toast to their tiny friends.

WHAT CHRISTMAS BROUGHT THE STRANGER

MARGARET E. SANGSTER

The little inland town of Antrim had long ceased to be glad when new people came to dwell in it. Unlike most places in America, it was not pushing, and the residents were not interested in, real estate, in the development of the locality, or in anything that savored especially of money. They were fortunate in having money enough for their wants, and they lived their simple lives in ample houses about which sweet old-fashioned gardens drowsed peacefully all winter under the snow, and bloomed gloriously all summer in a riot of flowers.

One mansion had been vacant for a decade, the owner having died abroad leaving no heirs. Antrim people heard by and by with a little regret that the Sprague place had been purchased, and that it would presently be occupied by its new owner. This person turned out to be a middle-aged lady who arrived on a September morning with two maids and a servant. The long-closed house was opened and renovated. Painters and paperhangers from the nearest city came and went; the grounds were put in order, and the house very soon lost the air of neglect that had invested it so long.

The minister's wife was entertaining a group of the church ladies one afternoon in early October and, just before the circle broke up, suggested that as the minister and herself had called upon Mrs. Whitfield at the Sprague place, she thought it would be kind if the friends in the congregation would follow their example.

"Mrs. Whitfield," she said, "appears to be a quiet, refined woman of wealth and culture. She will be an acquisition to us, and she has already taken a pew and is coming to our church."

"What did you think of her? I don't mean what did you think about her education, her manners, and her clothes, but about herself?" asked Mrs. Fawcett. My husband says that she has not brought any letters of introduction, and he does not believe that she wants to make acquaintances."

"Everybody wants to make acquaintances," said the minister's wife with decision. "I thought Mrs. Whitfield very nice, a little quaint and old-fashioned and rather silent, but nice."

Acting on this hint, the good women of Antrim made calls by ones and twos and threes on Mrs. Whitfield, who received them graciously, but who did not seem to have very much ability in conversation. She was shy and reserved, and was somehow wrapped in a veil of sadness, as though something were on her mind. The minister's wife learned after a while that she had been a widow for twenty years, had lived long in Italy, and that two years before coming to Antrim she had lost her only child.

Mrs. Whitfield returned the calls that were made upon her, and she came regularly to church, but as the autumn weeks sped by it grew evident that she was not to be included, partly through her own fault and partly through the absorption of the Antrim people in their own affairs. She was an outsider, and in her case to be an outsider meant to be very lonely and to pass time in unfriendly solitude. Her maids grew weary of the seclusion of their exile and went back to town. Mrs. Whitfield sent for others, but failed to find anyone who would stay, and on Christmas Eve she sat alone beside her fire, grateful that her faithful servant, Robert, was loyal enough to stay by her and help her in whatever work was to be done.

A storm was brewing and the snow was beginning to fall in thick flakes. The room in which Mrs. Whitfield sat was very bright and cheery. Books and magazines lay on the table, and Robert brought in the supper he had prepared. As he set the tray on the table he smiled and glanced about the room with pleasure.

"It has a look of Christmas," said Robert.

"Yes, indeed," she answered, "thanks to you, Robert. But why in the world you thought of bringing a Christmas tree and setting it over there between the windows, when there's nobody here to enjoy it, I just can't make out."

"We never had a Christmas without a Christmas tree," he answered. "You're here, Miss Mary, and lots of memories—and the Christ child."

As he spoke, the bell at the front door rang loudly. Mrs. Whitfield started and looked up in surprise. "Who can it be?" she said.

"Maybe a telegram," said old Robert, "or a letter or folks from across the water. I'll go and open the door."

She listened to his steps on the polished floor of the hall and presently heard him talking with someone who seemed urgent and pleading. She followed Robert to the door. Three people were standing there, and one carried a bundle. A little old man, a little old woman, and a young girl. It was the girl in whose arms was the bundle. Robert closed the door, leaving them outside.

"Why, Robert," exclaimed Mrs. Whitfield, "open the door directly. This is no night to shut people out in the cold."

He did as she bade him, but his look was doubtful. He had no liking for tramps, and in his opinion the travelers belonged under that designation. The old woman and the young girl were silent, though all came in at Mrs. Whitfield's invitation. The old man spoke in a faint voice, but with crisp accents, and with something in his tones that made Mrs. Whitfield think of English cottagers who had been her neighbors in Sussex.

"We have lost our way, lady. We thought we were on the road to Fairview; but we've missed it, and our money is almost spent and we've nowhere to go, and seeing your light we thought maybe you'd give us shelter in the barn till tomorrow morning."

"I'm so glad you came here," said Mrs. Whitfield. "It's Christmas Eve and I wanted company. Let me see the baby. Come in, all of you, and sit down. Robert, get some supper for these friends. What's the use of my having a home if I can't entertain Christmas guests?"

She made the old man and the old woman sit down by the fire, helped them remove their wraps, then took the baby in her own arms while the baby's mother, a girl not twenty, leaned back in an armchair and fell fast asleep.

Their story was easily told. These immigrants from England were on their way to Fairview, a factory town some ten miles off. They had taken the train in the wrong direction and had spent all they dared of the little capital with which they were to begin a new home in a strange land. It had not seemed impossible earlier in the day for them to walk to their destination, but they were unused to the road and to the cutting cold and keen, snow-laden air. When they reached Antrim they were exhausted and did not know how to find lodging for the night.

In earlier times, and in some regions in this country still, hospitality was and is never refused to benighted travelers. In Antrim it would have been considered unsafe and indiscreet to the last degree to admit within one's doors three or four poor people who came out of space.

Mrs. Whitfield, whom everyone had thought cold and formal, who had finally been called "the stranger" by everyone in the village, was contradicting every Antrim theory. She held the baby close to her breast, and when its little

head lay against her, she felt happier than she had felt since Edith's eyes had closed and she had been left alone. When her visitors had been warmed and fed and had sat by the fire until they were rested, she led the way to her guest chambers, and there made them welcome to luxurious beds.

"God bless you, lady," said the old man, as he and his old wife said good night.

Mrs. Whitfield helped the young mother undress, and saw her and the baby made comfortable. The grandmother had told Mrs. Whitfield that the girl was a widow, and that the child had been born after its father's death.

Mrs. Whitfield went softly downstairs, stopping in her own room to rummage in a bureau drawer. From its depths she extracted a long white box. Opening it, she lifted with gentle hands one little frock after another, sheer and soft and trimmed with lace; and, taking little shoes and little socks, turned and went back to the room she had left. The young mother was kneeling by the bed. She rose as Mrs. Whitfield entered.

"You tell me that you came," Mrs. Whitfield said, "from Sussex? Were you born at such a place?" The lady named a little hamlet where she had spent several years when her daughter was a child. "Yes," was the answer.

"Do you remember a lady and a little girl who lodged with your mother? Perhaps you were too young to remember. The little girl's name was Edith, and she played with you and liked you better than her doll. I was not quite sure until I thought it all over a moment ago, when it came to me like a flash. I must be altered

or your father and mother would have known me. Here, dear, take these things. They are for your baby.

The next morning, Christmas morning, as they sat at breakfast, Mrs. Whitfield recalled herself to the old man and woman, whose wayfaring feet had led them to her door.

"You are really my friends," she said, "and I am going to keep you with me here in this lonesome, empty house, until the winter is gone and the bright, beautiful spring has come again. Christmas has brought to me, a stranger in this place, a bit of the life I had when I was young."

The people in Antrim never discovered how it was that the quaint old husband and wife and the pretty young woman and lovely babe, who were established in Mrs. Whitfield's home as if they were kith and kin, came to her that Christmas Eve. She kept her own counsel, and Robert was no gossip. They came and they stayed. That was all Antrim people ever knew; but the merry Christmas they brought made Mrs. Whitfield so motherly and dear that she ceased to be a stranger and became everybody's friend.

CHRISTMAS MEMORIES

THE CHRISTMAS FEAST

ANDREW WARD

All Christmas morning long my grandfather's house used to breathe the sleepy steam of roasting turkey. As we opened our presents, one at a time in the dappled glow of tree and hearth, Grandma's confections would already be circulating: almond crescents, addictive candied grapefruit rind, balls of chopped apricot rolled in sugar.

Now and then Grandma and Grandpa would be summoned from the tree by chattering timers to baste the turkey, reset the oven, put the sweet potatoes in to bake. And when all the presents were opened, Grandpa commenced what we called the "center-ring cooking," decked out ostentatiously in an apron, sipping conspicuously from the mixing spoons, conducting with the baster.

"There's a lion in my kitchen," Grandma would declare as he worked at a portion of the counter he'd roped off for his artistry. Grandpa was a man of firm culinary convictions: about the consistency of gravy, the buoyancy of boiled onions, the clarity of roasting juices. But truth be known, he was merely the figurehead; my grandmother was the steady driving piston of the Christmas kitchen engine—paring, chopping, sautéing, stewing—a juggler of eggs and mixer blades and any grandchildren who insisted on making themselves useful.

A showboat exacts a certain toll from the rest of the fleet, and when the time came to carve the turkey, Grandpa was all theatrics and craft. He would make certain we were already seated with our eyes fixed on the kitchen door before he would shoulder his way into the dining room carrying the grand brown bird on a heavy silver tray festooned with parsley.

He would lead us in grace; a brief and ambiguous, "Our Father, we thank Thee, Amen," and then he would ask which of us wanted breast or thigh.

My grandfather Ward was an architectural historian and possessed, by his count, America's second largest collection of F. AD. Richter & Co. stone building blocks, with which at Christmastime he used to construct winter scenes on the mantelpiece and cabinet tops of his large, chock-a-block house in Oberlin, Ohio.

His holiday masterpiece was the stone village he erected in the center of the dining table, including church and school and cemetery, dusted with false snow and minutely flanked by wire and bristle stands of pines. It was a village such as Dickens might have traveled in his dreams, and so perfect that, as I peered at it street level around the crystal stems of water glasses and along the tines of silver forks, I would not have been too surprised if Scrooge himself had appeared in a tiny doorway, stamping the powder from his boots.

Grandpa was always generous with strangers. "I am Clarence Ward and this is my family," he would have told Ebenezer, showing him to a perch on the salt cellar. "Someone pass Mr. Scrooge the relish tray."

"Now go ahead and start in," Grandpa always told us, poking at the air with a flesh fork as he doled out the slices of breast meat that seemed to fall from his knife like pages from a book. "Don't wait for me. It'll just get cold."

And so we would all start in, passing the cranberries over the china and silver and crystal, perhaps grazing the precarious stone steeples. But by the time Grandpa had finally served himself, and all the fixings had been passed around again for his benefit, his eagle eye would alight on a grandson's already empty plate.

"Geoff? It looks as though you could do with a little more turkey."

"Yes, thank you, Grandpa," my brother would say, passing his plate. "It's all delicious."

"That's the boy," Grandpa replied, bending over the shredded bird. "Of course," he muttered, "I haven't had my first bite yet."

We would debate the vices and virtues of faculty politics and the fruit harvest just past and the route we took to get there, while we consumed the white meat and dark meat and the yams and creamed onions and gravy and stuffing and cranberries and relishes, and then the plum pudding flaming blue and gold, with hard sauce. And when the dishes were done and the narcotic of turkey and hard sauce had kicked in, the adults dozed and we children dawdled, sated, in the far-flung reaches of the house.

The wiring was poor in my grandparents' house, and so the light was dim and rosy; and even if it was not so dim and rosy, it appears that way in the old slides Grandpa left behind as a proud record of his holiday productions. And so that is the glow my memory casts on all my holiday expectations, soft and hibernal and benign.

My father's carving was crippled by irony. He'd been his father's stagehand all his boyhood and had neither Grandpa's taste for the spotlight nor his knack with a carving knife. One year I saw a woman on television demonstrate how to carve a turkey. Remove the wings and legs first, she instructed, and then, starting on the leg end of the bird, carve the breast meat backward. So I passed this along to my father, who hates instructions, and he duly removed the legs and wings and set them aside. But when he turned back to carve he couldn't for the life of him figure out where the wings had been and where the legs had been, and none of the rest of us could either. And so he guessed: badly, as it turned out, for the breast meat came off in shreds.

But it was on my parents' rooftop, not my grandparents', that I heard, indisputably, one Christmas Eve, the runners of Santa's sleigh. And it was along my parents' table that I saw the family ebb and flow. First my brother's wife appeared at a chair beside my father, and then my nephew Nathan and my niece Kelly moved from high chairs to center chairs along the tablesides. And

Christmas Eve.

then my wife Debbie sat herself to my father's left, and then Grandpa asked to be excused, giving his chair to my son Jake. And then Grandma left us too, and along came my daughter Casey.

My clan is composed of some of the most ferociously autonomous people I know, but there is something about the family feast that emulsifies us. Maybe it's because it requires that each of us be so many different things at once. In my case I must be son and little brother and big brother and brother-in-law and uncle and husband and father, in alternation or combination, depending on the seating arrangement. I may play uncle superbly with my niece, but my wife will think I'm reverting while my father will think I'm putting on airs.

Trying to be myself with the whole clan gathered is a more or less hopeless proposition. In this respect the roles of patriarch and matriarch are probably the least complicated, because everyone else is expecting more or less the same thing from them. It's the rest of us who must flirt with schizophrenia, floundering for perches on the flimsy outer branches of the family tree.

Even if we have seen each other once or twice a week over the past year, we are expected to behave as though this were an annual reunion. We bring to the holiday a collision of agendas, and occasionally someone will retreat in tears or wander muttering into the yard: perhaps no one touched the fruit cake, or the tree lights went on the blink, or we jubilated too halfheartedly singing carols by the tree. With fourteen of us jammed together, the holiday feast and all its surrounding rituals seemed almost a setup sometimes, a guarantee that

someone somehow was bound to be disappointed.

For our first Christmas alone together in the Great Northwest, Debbie and the kids and I bought a little Douglas fir. Out of a belief, I think, that the familiar would only remind us of the strangeness of our new surroundings, we displaced the traditional turkey with a slab of king salmon barbecued on the deck in the mild northwestern winter damp. And to this interloper at the family feast Debbie added her mother's persimmon pudding and corn bread, and our neighbors joined us, bearing pies for dessert.

My own children probably won't remember this first northwestern Christmas in their dreams. Their dreams of Christmas shall always be of their grandparents' Christmas: jostling among their cousins in the path of my mother's Yuletide snowball, glimpsing their own destinies in the postures and poses and crotchets of their kin. But now I wonder if in my turn I might yet become holiday impresario to my own grandchildren, and exist beyond my lifetime in the same rosy, retrospective glow.

But now I hear Debbie's timer ringing, and I must join the family at the table. So blessings on you, and the constancy of family and the abidance of friends, and whichever of the winter lights you praise.

PIONEERS IN MAINE

JOHN GOULD

They came up here in the early spring, just too late to get the full run of the maple sap, and Great-grandfather had hardly gotten his kettle set up when the run was over. They cleared a strip, and when the wind was right, burned to it, prodding their seeds into the ember-warm loam with sharp sticks. They had brought all their belongings in an ox cart, slashing a road ahead of the steers through forests that had never felt an ax before. They slept under the cart the first night they got here, and the next day Great-grandfather made a brush lean-to until the gardens were in.

That summer he chopped at the old-growth pines that towered over the Ridge—and he told afterward how he jumped the yoke of oxen onto a stump and turned them around without stepping off. He rigged a chain so the oxen would gee and roll a log, and he laid up a cabin as the summer advanced. He laid poles around through the woods and so made a pasture for the cow and pig. The oxen and hens lived in brush shelters. Great-grandmother didn't have a bed to sleep in until late in July, and the chimney wasn't laid up until September. The prospects of a long winter were nothing to cheer their spirits.

Great-grandmother was only eighteen then, and Great-grandfather was only nineteen, and they would be alone in their wilderness cabin now until the alders budded again and some trader would paddle up after the freshet to see what skins he could buy. Six months, at least; and maybe the trader wouldn't come then, and Jacob would have to leave her alone for a few days while he took his skins down himself. . . .

Great-grandmother was moody by times, and Great-grandfather was sympathetic and understanding—but what could he do about it? A woman likes to have another woman to "set" with now and again, and a windowless cabin surrounded by towering white pines that moan in the wind isn't the best thing in the world to cure lonesomeness. Another year or so, and things would be different, but for the time being, the whole world was whittled down to a half-acre of snow in an unbroken forest of pine.

Then one fine morning in early December, Great-grandfather went out in the quiet frost of sunrise and shielded his eyes against the east. Over on the other rim of the intervale, a thin column of smoke rose into the sun. Smoke in the woods is something to investigate, but he didn't say anything about it in the cabin. He milked, had breakfast, and picked up his ax as if to go on clearing away big trees. But he circled the clearing and

headed down towards Little River, climbed up on the other side, and soon could hear an ax ringing against frozen timber.

It was ringing for fair. Great-grandfather came out into a clearing just as a mighty pin teetered, swayed, gathered momentum, and crashed to the ground with a torrent of thunder that echoed throughout the forest. A pint-sized man in deerskin thereupon leaped onto the stump, sunk his ax in the trunk of the tree, waved his hat and cheered at his own triumph.

Great-grandfather smiled, because he knew how it felt to get one more tree out of the way. The cheering brought a woman out of a hut at the far end of the clearing, and she waved at the pint-sized man and cheered with him.

Great-grandfather practically frightened the two when he began cheering as well, for until that moment they had believed themselves alone in the great Bowdoin grant. They shook hands, and Great-grandfather was invited to stay and break bread, but he couldn't because Great-

grandmother would be expecting him. But he did promise to come back on Christmas and bring his wife.

The pint-sized man had a voice like a bull, and he shouted, "We'll stew some venison and make Christmas worth remembering!"

The pint-sized man was a trapper, and he'd brought in food for the winter, so he hadn't needed the summer growing season. He'd come late in October, and until that morning he and Great-grandfather had each thought himself the first settler north of New Meadows. Great-grandfather sat breathless by the fire when he got home, and told all about his discovery—particularly about the woman Great-grandmother's age, and he imitated the little fellow with the big voice so Great-grandmother laughed aloud for the first time in weeks.

The news did wonders for her. She hummed and sang and finished her housework in half the time so she could be out with an ax and Great-grandfather, helping him limb the trees and talking about Christmas.

"What can we take them for a present?" she asked, well knowing the scarcity of her cabin.

"I know," she answered herself. "I'll make up a little sugar. We hain't much, but they hain't none, probably, and won't see none till spring."

So Great-grandfather fashioned a tiny wooden pail, staved from split pine and bound with willow. He found some black alder berries, and Great-grandmother made a fir spray that served as a cover. She pounded out a cake of sugar, and twice decided she had enough, and twice went up the ladder for a doit more.

Great-grandfather, pleased with the tiny wooden pail, immediately made several big ones for Great-grandmother's Christmas present, and then decided to take one as a gift to his hostess. But his real present to Great-grandmother was a swing-dingle—for he wanted her to go calling in style.

How America has disintegrated, when a swing-dingle must be explained! It was a white maple trunk, the right size, and properly curved in growing so the turned-up end made a runner. The top was split its length, with a tree nail at the proper place to stop its splitting all the way. The split part fitted like fills to a steer, and over the runner was erected a bobsled sort of seat on which Great-grandmother could, and did, ride to Christmas dinner.

Great-grandfather walked on ahead, teaming the single steer around blowdowns. At Little River, he walked out and tested the ice, and then he scooted Great-grandmother across so she nearly bounced off when the swing-dingle hit the opposite bank. Up the other hill they went, and the pint-sized man was sitting on a stump by his cabin watching for them.

"Here they come!" he called, and his wife rushed from the cabin as eager and expectant as Great-grandmother was. "Merry Christmas!" she called, and Great-grandfather waved his goad stick and called back, "Merry Christmas!"

"Merry Christmas," yelled the pint-sized man in his bull's voice, and Great-grandmother waved from her perch on the swing-dingle and said, "Merry Christmas!"

Then she added "Neighbor!"

THE RED MITTENS

ROSALYN HART FINCH

Christmas was coming and I was doing some heavy complaining to Mama about pocket money. "All the other kids in fifth grade are gonna buy their Christmas gifts," I said pointedly when Mama suggested that "homemade gifts are more love-filled than bought ones."

"How come we always have to be poor?" I grumbled.

"Being poor has nothing to do with giving," said Mama. "It's not what you give, but how you give."

But I didn't agree. Christmas week was unseasonably warm for Ohio, turning the month-long layers of snow into messy puddles and slush. But things began looking up for me; I had an idea.

Early on Saturday morning I bundled up my five-year-old brother, Dicky, who owned the one and only wagon on the block, jammed my way into my mackinaw, shoved on boots and gloves, emptied the wagon of Dicky's junk, and took off with Dicky in it.

Across the backyard and through the stubbled cornfield that edged along the rear of our property and spread as far as our eyes could see, I trotted, pulling Dicky and the wagon behind me.

At last, reaching the train tracks bordering the cornfield, I unfolded my plan to Dicky. "What we're gonna do, Dicky, is load the wagon with all the hunks of coal we can find beside the tracks. Then we'll take it to the gas station and sell it."

"For money?" Dicky's eyes widened. "Will I get some too?"

"Sure," I promised. "We both will."

"Oh, boy," Dicky scuttled out of the wagon, eager to begin. "How'd this stuff get here?" he asked, stooping to brush the remaining slush from a chunk of "black gold."

"It falls off the trains," I cried happily, tossing chunks into the wagon as fast as I could pick them up. I'd never dreamed there'd be so much.

In short order we had stacked a small black mountain and were headed toward the gas station, Dicky pushing and me pulling. By the time we'd reached the road to the station, Dicky was whining and crying, filled with cold and fatigue.

An old woman I'd often seen at church, Mrs. Scott, was out sweeping the slush from her front porch. "What's wrong, children?" she called.

"Nothing," I yelled back. "My brother's just cold."

"Why don't you bring him inside by the stove? I could fix you both some hot cocoa."

Dicky ran to the offered haven. Much as I would have loved a little warmth and some cocoa, I declined. I was anxious to get the money the coal would bring me. I left Dicky and said I'd be back.

Puffing and blowing, I trudged the rest of the way alone. My numb feet were stumbling at everything and my fingers burned. My heart hit bottom when the gas station man said, "Didn't cha' notice the weather's turned? We ain't buying any more coal. We're full up."

Tears of disappointment stung my eyes as I grabbed the wagon handle and ran back, tears streaming down my face. How I arrived at Mrs. Scott's house again I don't recall.

"Dicky has to go home now," I managed to say, looking down at the ground.

"Whatever's the matter, dear?" Mrs. Scott said, drawing me gently inside and wiping my tear-stained face with her apron. "Come by the kitchen stove for some cocoa."

Dicky pulled my sleeve. "Didja get the money?" he jabbered, holding out a ready hand.

That did it. I sobbed out my disappointment. "There isn't any money. The gas station man wouldn't buy the coal."

When I lifted my head to wipe my tears, Mrs. Scott held out a steaming cup of cocoa. "What a shame, dear. Dicky told me how hard you both worked."

I nodded. "I was counting on it for a Christmas present for my class exchange."

Mrs. Scott kept shaking her head, clucking sympathetically. Then her face brightened. She hurried over to the cupboard, reached up to the top shelf, and lifted down an ancient yellowing teapot. Pulling off the lid, she dumped out a dollar bill, a dime, and a nickel.

"Would this be enough to buy your coal?" she asked, spreading it out on the table.

Money! My eyes fairly leapt at the sight of it, then lingered on Mrs. Scott's hands as they smoothed out the dollar bill. They were red and rough. I raised my eyes and for the first time noticed the patch on her apron and the faded kitchen curtains and the newspaper taped to the windows. My heart sank. She couldn't really spare the money for the coal.

A pile of bright red mittens sat on the countertop. I looked at them curiously. "I just knitted those for our missionary society," she said. "Here, try a pair." They were much too big for me, but I didn't let on.

"They're beautiful," I said. "I'll trade you the coal for a pair of mittens, Mrs. Scott."

"Would you really like them?" asked Mrs. Scott. I nodded.

"I think we've made a fine exchange," she beamed as she pulled her sweater about her shoulders. It was chilly away from the stove. . . .

I ended up giving one of Mama's "homemade gifts" for my class gift exchange that year, and I kept Mrs. Scott's snug red mittens for myself. Her gift warmed my hands all winter long; and more importantly, my heart was warmed whenever I thought of my gift of coal to her.

Mama was right. Love-filled gifts are the best.

COUNTRY CHRISTMAS

WILLA CATHER

During the week before Christmas, Jake was the most important person of our household, for he was to go to town and do all our Christmas shopping. But on the twenty-first of December, the snow began to fall. The flakes came down so thickly that from the sitting-room windows I could not see beyond the windmill—its frame looked dim and grey, unsubstantial like a shadow. The snow did not stop falling all day, or during the night that followed. The cold was not severe, but the storm was quiet and resistless. The men could not go farther than the barns and corral. They sat about the house most of the day as if it were Sunday; greasing their boots, mending their suspenders, plaiting whiplashes.

On the morning of the twenty-second, Grandfather announced at breakfast that it would be impossible to go to Black Hawk for Christmas purchases. We decided to have a country Christmas, without any help from town. Fuchs got out the old candle molds and made tallow candles. Grandmother hunted up her fancy cake-cutters and baked gingerbread men and roosters, which we decorated with burnt sugar and red cinnamon drops.

On the day before Christmas, Jake packed the things we were sending to the Shimerdas in his saddle bags and set off on Grandfather's gray gelding. That afternoon I watched long and eagerly from the sitting-room window. At last I saw a dark spot moving on the west hill, beside the half-buried cornfield, where the sky was taking on a coppery flush from the sun that did not quite break through. I put on my cap and ran out to meet Jake. When I got to the pond, I could see that he was bringing in a little cedar tree across his pommel. He not forgotten how much I liked them.

By the time we had placed the cold, fresh-smelling little tree in a corner of the sitting room, it was already Christmas Eve. After supper we all gathered there, and even Grandfather, reading his paper by the table, looked up with friendly interest now and then. The cedar was about five feet high and very shapely. We hung it with the gingerbread animals, strings of popcorn, and bits of candle which Fuchs had fitted into pasteboard sockets. Its real splendors, however, came from the most unlikely place in the world—from Otto's cowboy trunk. I had never seen anything in that trunk but old boots and spurs and pistols, and a fascinating mixture of yellow leather thongs, cartridges, and shoemaker's wax. From under the lining he now produced a collection of brilliantly colored paper figures, several inches high and stiff enough to stand alone. They had been sent to him year after year, by his old mother in Austria. There was a bleeding heart, in tufts of paper lace; there were the three kings, gorgeously appareled, and the ox and the ass and the shepherds; there was the Baby in the manger, and a group of angels, singing; there were camels and leopards, held by the black slaves of the three kings. Our tree became the talking tree of the fairy tale; legends and stories nestled like birds in its branches. Grandmother said it reminded her of the Tree of Knowledge. We put sheets of cotton wool under it for a snowfield, and Jake's pocket mirror for a frozen lake.

On Christmas morning, when I got down to the kitchen, the men were just coming in from their morning chores—the horses and pigs always had their breakfast before we did. Jake and Otto shouted "Merry Christmas!" to me, and winked at each other when they saw the waffle irons on the stove.

Grandfather came down, wearing a white shirt and his Sunday coat. Morning prayers were longer than usual. He read the chapters from Saint Matthew about the birth of Christ, and as we listened, it all seemed like something that had happened lately, and near at hand.

In his prayer he thanked the Lord for the first Christmas, and for all that it had meant to the world ever since. He gave thanks for our food and comfort, and prayed for the poor and destitute in great cities, where the struggle for life was harder than it was here with us. Grandfather had the gift of simple and moving expression. Because he talked so little, his words had a peculiar force; they were not worn dull from constant use.

After we sat down to our waffles and sausage, Jake told us how pleased the Shimerdas had been with their presents; even Ambrosch was friendly and went to the creek with him to cut the Christmas tree. It was a soft gray day outside, with heavy clouds working across the sky, and occasional squalls of snow.

There were always odd jobs to be done about the barn on holidays, and the men were busy until afternoon. At about four o'clock a visitor appeared: Mr. Shimerda, wearing his rabbit-skin cap and collar, and new mittens his wife had knitted. He had come to thank us for the presents, and for all Grandmother's kindness to his family. Jake and Otto joined us from the basement and we sat about the stove, enjoying the deepening gray of the winter afternoon and the atmosphere of comfort and security in my grandfather's house.

This feeling seemed completely to take possession of Mr. Shimerda. The old man had come to believe that peace and order had vanished from the earth, or existed only in the old world he had left so far behind. He sat still and passive, his head resting against the back of the wooden rocking chair, his hands relaxed upon the arms. His face had a look of weariness and pleasure, like that of sick people when they feel relief from pain. He said almost nothing, and smiled rarely; but as he rested there we all had a sense of his utter content.

As it grew dark, I asked whether I might light the Christmas tree before the lamp was brought. When the candle ends sent up their conical yellow flames, all the colored figures from Austria stood out clearly and full of meaning against the green boughs. Mr. Shimerda rose, crossed himself, and quietly knelt down before the tree, his head sunk forward. His long body formed a letter 'S.' I saw Grandmother look apprehensively at Grandfather. He was rather narrow in religious matters, and sometimes spoke out and hurt people's feelings. There had been nothing strange about the tree before, but now, with someone kneeling before it—images, candles—Grandfather merely put his fingertips to his brow and bowed his venerable head.

We persuaded our guest to stay for supper with us. He needed little urging. As we sat down to the table, it occurred to me that he liked to look at us, and that our faces were open books to him. When his deep-seeing eyes rested on me, I felt as if he were looking far ahead into the future for me, down the road I would have to travel.

At nine o'clock Mr. Shimerda lighted one of our lanterns and put on his overcoat. He stood in the little entry hall, the lantern and his fur cap under his arm, shaking hands with us. When he took Grandmother's hand, he bent over it as he always did, and said slowly, "Good woman!" He made the sign of the cross over me, put on his cap and went off in the dark. As we turned back to the sitting room, Grandfather looked at me searchingly. "The prayers of all good people are good."

REMEMBERING THE WARMTH OF CHRISTMAS

❦ THE SEASON'S LOVE AND JOY FONDLY RECALLED ❦

Come, sing a hale heigh-ho
For the Christmas long ago!
When the old log cabin homed us
From the night of blinding snow,
Where the rarest joy held reign,
And the chimney roared amain,
With the firelight like a beacon
Through the frosty windowpane.

—JAMES WHITCOMB RILEY

But give me holly, bold and jolly,
Honest, prickly, shining holly;
Pluck me holly leaf and berry
For the day when I make merry.

—CHRISTINA G. ROSSETTI

So, now is come our joyful feast,
Let every soul be jolly!
Each room with ivy leaves is drest,
And every post with holly.

Though some churls at our mirth repine,
Round your brows let garlands twine,
Drown sorrow in a cup of wine,
And let us all be merry!

Now all our neighbors' chimneys smoke,
And Christmas logs are burning;
Their ovens with baked meats do choke,
And all their spits are turning.

Without the door let sorrow lie,
And if for cold it hap to die,
We'll bury it in Christmas pie,
And evermore be merry!

—GEORGE WITHER

When Christmas fires gleam and glow,

Christmas is coming; the goose is getting fat.
Please to put a penny in the old man's hat.
If you haven't got a penny, a ha'penny will do.
If you haven't got a ha'penny, then God bless you.

—Author Unknown

On Christmas Eve the bells were rung;
The damsel donned her kirtle sheen;
The hall was dressed with holly green;
Forth to the wood did merry men go,
To gather in the mistletoe.

—Sir Walter Scott

Let every hall have boughs of green,
With berries growing in between,
In the week when Christmas comes.

—Eleanor Farjeon

The holly and the ivy,
Now they are full well grown,
Of all the trees that are in the wood,
The holly bears the crown.

The holly bears a blossom,
As white as the lily flower,
And Mary bore sweet Jesus Christ
To be our sweet Savior.

—Medieval English Carol

'Tis merry 'neath the mistletoe,
When holy berries glisten bright;
When Christmas fires gleam and glow;
When wintry winds so wildly blow;

And all the meadows round are white—
'Tis merry 'neath the mistletoe!
A privilege 'tis then, you know,
To exercise time-honored rite;

When Christmas fires gleam and glow,
When loving lips may pout, although
With other lips they oft unite—
'Tis merry 'neath the mistletoe!

—Joseph Ashby-Sterry

hen wintry winds so wildly blow . . .

THE CHRISTMAS
STORY RETOLD

AMAHL AND THE NIGHT VISITORS

GIAN CARLO MENOTTI

usic from a shepherd's pipe filled the cold winter air. Wrapped in a heavy cloak, a boy sat in the evening shadow, piping steadily. As he played, stars appeared in the darkening sky. The boy could see that one star burned more brightly than the others, and he could not take his eyes from it. He did not hear his mother call him from the small house nearby.

A moment later, she called again. "Amahl! Time to go to bed!"

"Oh, very well." Amahl picked up the crutch lying beside him on the ground. Leaning on it heavily, he limped into the house. "What was keeping you outside?"

Amahl turned toward his mother. "Oh, Mother, you should go out and see! There's never been such a sky!" Amahl limped across the room, talking excitedly. "Hanging over our roof there is a star as large as a window. The star has a tail, and it moves across the sky like a chariot on fire."

Amahl's mother sighed. "Oh, Amahl," she said wearily, "when will you stop telling lies? All day long you wander about in a dream."

"Mother, I'm not lying," said Amahl. "Please believe me. There is a star," Amahl persisted, "and it has a tail this long." He held out his arms as wide as he could.

"Amahl." His mother's voice was reproving.

"Cross my heart and hope to die," Amahl said.

Putting her arms around her son, Amahl's mother said, "Poor Amahl, hunger has gone to your head. Unless we go begging how shall we live through tomorrow?" Amahl's mother wept. "My little son, a beggar!" she said.

"Don't cry, Mother dear, don't worry for me." Amahl knelt by her side. "If we must go begging, a good beggar I'll be. I'll play sweet tunes to set people dancing. We'll walk and walk from village to town, you dressed as a gypsy and I as a clown. I'll play my pipe, you'll sing and you'll shout. The windows will open and people will lean out. The king will ride by and hear your loud voice and throw us some gold to stop all the noise." Amahl and his mother tried to smile.

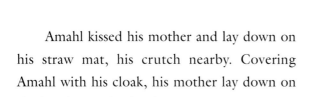

Amahl kissed his mother and lay down on his straw mat, his crutch nearby. Covering Amahl with his cloak, his mother lay down on the bench near the fireplace and was soon asleep.

Awake in the dark room, Amahl heard singing in the distance.

> From far away we come
> And farther we must go.
> How far, how far, my crystal star?

Amahl raised himself onto one elbow. The singing was closer.

> The shepherd dreams inside the fold.
> Cold are the sands by the silent sea.
> Frozen the incense in our frozen hands,
> Heavy the gold.

Amahl threw back his cloak, found his crutch, and hobbled to the window. At first he saw nothing, although the singing continued.

At the window, Amahl watched as a magnificent caravan approached his house. Three stately camels carrying three richly dressed men moved past Amahl at his window and then came to a stop.

There was a knock at the door.

Amahl's mother did not stir from the bench. "Amahl," she said, "go and see who's knocking at the door."

"Yes, Mother." Amahl hobbled to the door and opened it a crack. One of the richly dressed men from the caravan was standing before him. Up close, Amahl could see the man was wearing a crown. Amahl stared for a moment.

"Mother, Mother, Mother," Amahl called as he limped across the room, "come with me. I want to be sure you see what I see."

Sitting up, Amahl's mother asked, "What is the matter with you?"

"Mother," Amahl said hesitantly, "outside the door there is . . . there is a king with a crown!"

Amahl's mother seemed to be talking to the ceiling. "What shall I do with this boy? What shall I do?"

There was a second knock at the door. "Go back and see who it is and ask them what they want," Amahl's mother said, and she lay down once more.

Amahl hobbled to the door, looked out, and returned to his mother saying, "Mother, Mother, Mother, come with me." He paused. "If I tell you the truth, I know you won't believe me."

"I'll believe you if you tell the truth," said his mother.

Amahl took a deep breath. "There are three kings," he announced, "and one of them is black!"

"Oh! What shall I do with this boy!" Amahl's mother was very angry. "I'm going to the door myself, and then, young man, you'll have to reckon with me!"

As the door swung open, Amahl's mother gasped and then bowed low, for standing in the doorway were three men dressed in royal splendor. Each king carried a treasure: one a softly burnished chalice of myrrh, one a gleaming urn of incense, and one an elaborate coffer of gold.

"Good evening." They spoke together.

"May we rest awhile in your house and warm ourselves by your fireplace?" asked the black king.

"I am a poor widow. All I can offer you are a cold fireplace and a bed of straw. But to these you are welcome," Amahl's mother replied.

Bowing again, Amahl's mother said, "Come in, come in!"

A page, carrying a lantern, entered first. He was bent almost double under the baggage he carried on his back, which included an Oriental rug, a parrot in a cage, and a beautiful jeweled box.

"It is nice here," said Melchior, looking around the room.

"We can only stay a little while," said Melchior. "We must not lose sight of our star."

"Your star?" asked Amahl's mother.

"What did I tell you?" Amahl whispered to her.

"Are you a real king?" Amahl asked, leaning on his crutch.

"I live in a black marble palace, full of black panthers and white doves," said Balthazar. "And you, little boy, what do you do?"

"I was a shepherd," Amahl said sadly to Balthazar. "I had a flock of sheep, but my mother sold them. Now there are no sheep left."

"And what is this?" asked Amahl, pointing to the beautiful jeweled box.

Holding up the box and speaking with excitement, Kaspar said to Amahl, "This is my box, this is my box, I never travel without my box." He opened the top drawer. "In the first drawer I keep my magic stones." Kaspar held each stone in turn before Amahl's dazzled eyes and said, "One carnelian against all evil and envy, one moonstone to make you sleep, one red coral to heal your wounds, one lapis lazuli against winter fever, one small jasper to help you find water, one small topaz to soothe your eyes, and one red ruby to protect you from lightning."

Kaspar opened the next drawer. "In the second drawer I keep all my beads. In the third drawer . . ." He paused, and Amahl could hardly hear Kaspar as he said, "Oh, little boy, in the third drawer I keep . . ." Kaspar took a deep breath and smiled broadly at Amahl. "Licorice!" he said happily, "Black sweet licorice. Have some." He thrust the drawer at Amahl, who grabbed a piece and was swallowing the last of it when his mother returned.

"Amahl, I told you not to be a nuisance," she scolded.

"But it isn't my fault," Amahl protested. Then hobbling toward her, he whispered, "They kept asking me questions."

"I want you to go out and call the shepherds," said his mother. "Tell them about our visitors and ask them to bring whatever they have in their houses, as we have nothing to offer them. Hurry!"

"Yes, Mother." Amahl wrapped his cloak about him and put on his hat. Leaning on his crutch, he limped out as quickly as he could.

His mother moved toward the coffer of gold and the rich chalices of myrrh and incense spread out before the kings. "These beautiful things," she exclaimed, "and all that gold!"

"These are gifts to the Child," Melchior told her.

"The child?" asked Amahl's mother. "Which child?"

"We don't know," said Melchior. "But the Star will guide us to Him."

"Perhaps I know him," said Amahl's mother. "What does he look like?"

"Have you seen a child the color of wheat, the color of dawn?" asked Melchior. "His eyes are mild, and his hands are those of a king. We are bringing incense, myrrh, and gold to Him, and the Eastern Star is our guide."

Amahl's mother answered softly, "Yes, I know a child the color of wheat, the color of dawn. His eyes are mild, and his hands are those of a king. But no one will bring him incense or gold, though he may be sick and poor and hungry and cold." She paused for a moment. "He's my child, my son, my darling, my own."

Melchior stretched out a hand. "The Child we seek holds the seas and the winds on His palm," he said.

"The child we seek has the moon and the stars at His feet," said Kaspar.

And Balthazar added, "Before Him the eagle is gentle, the lion is meek."

Going to the door and looking out for Amahl, his mother said softly, "The child I know holds my hand on his palm, the child I know has my life at his feet. He's my child, my son, my darling, my own, and his name is Amahl."

The room became quiet—so quiet that Kaspar dozed off. Suddenly, a call was heard.

"The shepherds are coming," Amahl's mother told the kings.

The shepherds crowded into the doorway of Amahl's house.

"Oh! Look! Look!" they said to each other. They were so overcome by the splendor of the kings, they felt afraid to enter.

From the center of the group one man approached the kings. He bowed and set a tray before them. "Olives and quinces, apples and raisins, nutmeg and myrtle, persimmons and chestnuts—this is all we shepherds can offer you.

"Thank you, thank you, thank you kindly," said the three kings in unison.

A second shepherd approached the kings and, after bowing, set another tray before them. "Citrons and lemons, musk and pomegranates, goat cheese and walnuts, figs and cucumbers, this is all we shepherds can offer you," the man said to the kings.

"Thank you, thank you, thank you kindly," the kings said, again speaking as one.

"Take them, eat them, you are welcome," said a shepherd to the kings, while another shepherd repeated to the page, "Take them, eat them, you are welcome too."

"Thank you, good friends, for your gifts. But now we must bid you good night. We have little time for sleep and a long journey tomorrow."

Bowing as they passed before the kings, the shepherds filed out of Amahl's house.

In the house, the kings settled themselves for sleep near the fireplace. Amahl and his mother on their pallets, the three kings huddled together, and the page curled up on the rug near the gold, listened as the shepherds' last notes lingered in the stillness. Soon nearly everyone was asleep.

Amahl's mother was awake, sitting stiffly on her pallet, staring at the treasure guarded by the page.

"All that gold!" she thought. "I wonder if rich people know what to do with their gold?" Amahl's mother raised herself to her knees and moved closer to the gold. "Oh, what I could do for my child with that gold! Why," she asked herself, "should it all go to a child they don't even know?" She crept even closer to the riches.

"They are asleep. Do I dare? If I take some, they'll never miss it."

She stretched herself toward the gold,

murmuring, "For my child . . . for my child . . . for my child . . ."

In an instant the page was awake. He grabbed Amahl's mother, shouting to the kings, "Thief, thief!" Her hands full of gold and jewels, Amahl's mother tried to free herself from the page, and the two of them dragged each other into the center of the room, fighting all the while.

"What is it?" asked the kings, rising from the bench in confusion.

"I've seen her steal some of the gold," the page panted as he struggled with Amahl's mother. "She's a thief! She's stolen the gold!"

"Shame! Shame!" the kings cried.

"Give it back, or I'll tear it out of you," snarled the page.

Frantically, Amahl hobbled to Kaspar and tugged on his robe. "Oh, don't let him hurt my mother! My mother is good. She cannot do anything wrong. I'm the one who lies. I'm the one who steals."

As fast as he could, Amahl limped back to the page, shouting, "Don't you dare hurt my mother! I'll break all your bones! I'll bash in your head!"

Melchior stood over the two of them. "Oh, woman," he said, "you may keep the gold. The Child we seek doesn't need our gold. He will build His Kingdom on love alone. His hand will not hold a scepter, His head will not wear a crown. His might will not be built by your toil." Melchior turned to Kaspar and Balthazar. "Let us leave, my friends."

Amahl's mother rushed toward the kings and knelt before them, spilling the gold she had taken onto the floor.

Christmas Joy with thee be found And Heavenly Peace thy heart surround

"Oh, no, wait—take your gold! I've waited all my life for such a king. And if I weren't so poor, I would send a gift of my own to such a child."

"Mother," said Amahl, "let me send Him my crutch. Who knows, He may need one, and this I made myself." Amahl offered his crutch to the kings.

Horrified, his mother said, "But you can't!" as Amahl, with his crutch still raised, took a step forward. A hush fell over the room. Holding his crutch in his outstretched hands, Amahl took another step. Breaking the silence Amahl whispered, "I walk, Mother. Mother, I walk!"

"He walks," said the three kings, together.

"He walks!" said Amahl's mother, rising to her feet, never taking her eyes from Amahl as he advanced steadily toward the kings, holding his crutch before him. As he placed it in Kaspar's hands, the three kings spoke. "It is a sign from the Holy Child. We must give praise to the newborn King."

Amahl walked to the center of the room. At first his steps were slow, but soon he moved faster. "Look, Mother, I can dance, I can jump, I can run!" he called.

"Truly, he can dance, he can jump, he can run," the three kings echoed.

His mother ran after Amahl, afraid he might fall and hurt himself. When he stumbled, his mother quickly caught him, saying, "Please, my darling, be careful now. You must not hurt yourself."

"Oh, good woman, you must not be afraid," the kings told her, "for he is loved by the Son of God."

Kaspar stepped forward. "Oh, blessed child, may we touch you?" he asked. Amahl nodded yes. The three kings passed before Amahl and laid their hands on his head. Then each king picked up his gift to the Christ Child and prepared to leave.

Oh, Mother, let me go with the kings. I want to take my crutch to the Child myself."

"Yes, good woman, let him come with us," the kings said. "We'll take good care of him, and we'll bring him home on a camel's back."

Putting her arms around Amahl, his mother asked, "Do you really want to go?"

"Yes, Mother," said Amahl.

"Yes," she said, smiling at him, "I think you should go and bring thanks to the Child yourself."

Surprised, Amahl asked, "Are you sure?"

"Go on, get ready," his mother said, and Amahl hurried away to collect what he needed for his journey.

"Wash your ears," she said.

"Yes, I promise."

"Don't tell lies."

"No, I promise."

Softly, Amahl and his mother said to each other, "I shall miss you very much."

The caravan waited outside the house. On their camels, the kings looked more imposing than ever. Amahl hurried back to his mother to say goodbye one more time. Then the page helped him onto Kaspar's camel. With jingling bridles, the camels moved forward. Amahl waved to his mother. She waved back.

The caravan turned a corner, and Amahl could no longer see his mother or his house. Leaning against Kaspar, he brought out his shepherd's pipe and began to play.

REJOICING IN THE BIRTH OF OUR SAVIOR

❀ THE AMAZING GIFT FROM GOD TO MEN ❀

Bid them come not, as of old,
With frankincense, myrrh, gems and gold,
But with the nobler, love's own proffer—
Unto their God their hearts to offer.

—KATHLEEN KAVANAGH

Glorious now behold Him arise,
King and God and Sacrifice;
Alleluia, Alleluia,
Earth to heav'n replies.

O star of wonder, star of night,
Star with royal beauty bright,
Westward leading, still proceeding,
Guide us to thy perfect light.

—JOHN HENRY HOPKINS JR.

Given, not lent,
But not withdrawn—once sent,
This infant of mankind, this one,
Is still the little welcome Son.

—ALICE MEYNELL

And the star rains its fire while the beautiful sing,

For unto us a child is born, unto us a son is given:
and the government shall be upon his shoulder:
And his name shall be called Wonderful, Counsellor, The mighty God,
The everlasting Father, The Prince of Peace.

—Isaiah 9:6

The gift of love in Mary's eyes,
Looked down on Jesus with surprise,
That one so great should be so small,
To point the way for kings, and all.

One heart of love can move the race,
One grain of truth can change Earth's face,
A Bethlehem babe, a shepherd's rod,
Have lifted mankind up to God.

—Clarence Hawkes

There's a song in the air!
There's a star in the sky!
There's a mother's deep prayer
And a baby's low cry!

And the star rains its fire while the beautiful sing,
For the manger of Bethlehem cradles a king.

—Josiah Gilbert Holland

For once, on a December night,
An angel held a candle bright.
And led three wise men by its light
To where a Child was sleeping.

—Harriet F. Blodgett

for the manger of Bethlehem cradles a king.

SHEPHERDS AT THE BACK DOOR

FULTON OURSLER

Mary had fallen asleep, and there was quiet in the stable. Anna and Joachim made a bed for themselves, far back in the shadows. And Jesus, the baby, lay asleep in his first bed, which was the food box of the donkeys and the cows—a manger which the foster father had hastily filled with fresh hay and barley oats that smelled sweet and clean.

For Joseph, sleep was impossible. His mind, his very soul, was too tremulous and excited. Again he paced in a kind of march around the stable, stopping regularly to see that Mary and her child still breathed, which they did, quite naturally. There was glee in Joseph, a sacred rippling joy in his blood, a bounce to his muscles. His only regret was that he had no one to talk to; Joseph, in that dark hour, could have poured out his heart in rapturous conversation.

"The oddest thing about it," he told himself, in the absence of any companion, "was the feeling I had when I looked into that little fellow's eyes. I seemed to have known him all my life. He wasn't a stranger!"

Was that a special fact because Jesus was a special child? Because, after all, Joseph was not the child's father, and even now he did not allow himself to forget it. Yet he felt a tender closeness to the baby, deeper and truer than fatherhood itself. He still felt baffled that there was no further sign.

A long time had passed while Mary carried her baby, with no reassurance from supernatural beings. Nine months since the angel had stood with folded wings in the Nazareth house; the day of the Annunciation. After that the dream message had come to Joseph, then silence—months of commonplace reality. Was it not strange that the baby had been born without some demonstration? Here was the child; where were the angels?

He listened for a rustling of wings and heard only the sleepy bleat of a yearling lamb. That, and presently a low rumble of distant voices, the shuffling of feet outside the house and, at the lower back entrance of the stable, the knocking of a staff.

With a gasp of concern that Mary would be awakened, Joseph hurried to the door.

Unfastening the latch, he opened the upper half of the door, then put a finger warningly to his mouth. A group of bearded faces was staring at him. One man held up a lighted lantern. Behind them was still the night, dark and clear, with the sparkle of unaccountably and extraordinarily brilliant stars. Joseph had not seen those stars until now.

"Peace!" breathed Joseph. "This is no time to make noise."

"The Lord be unto you," returned one of the men in a low, placating voice. "We have not come to make any trouble at all."

"Who are you, then?"

"We are shepherds from the hills outside this town. We have been tending our flocks."

"The hour is late," insisted Joseph firmly.

He would have closed the door but the speaker held up his staff.

"Wait. Only one question. Has a child just been born in this place?"

A quiver of alarm passed through Joseph. Was something wrong? Their papers not in order, perhaps? Had they broken the law in taking shelter in the stable? No one ever knew what queer laws might be declared by King Herod.

"Why do you ask, shepherd? How is it your business about a child?"

"Don't be afraid of us. We are friends."

"Well, then, yes. A child has been born."

"Only a little while ago?"

"True. Within two hours."

Low exclamations came from the bearded mouths of the shepherds. They turned and patted one another on the back and one of them whispered, "It is true, then."

And the first speaker laid a kindly hand on Joseph's shoulder, "Tell me—is it a man-child?"

"It is."

"And could it be possible that you have laid the child in a manger?"

"Yes," answered Joseph, feeling the tears gather in his eyes. "There was no cradle, you see. The town is overcrowded; there was nowhere else I could take my lady. . . ."

"Then God be praised!" murmured the shepherd fervently, and the others muttered agreement in their beards.

"Listen, man," cried the one with the lifted staff. "We have just seen a marvelous sight. An unbelievable sight. And it has to do with you."

Marvelous sight! And unbelievable. Hope sprang up in Joseph's thoughts.

"Believe this thing we tell you: We were all tending our flocks tonight, minding our own business. The night was clear, air cool, stars bright, everything going along just as usual. Suddenly Jonas here interrupted our talk and pointed at the sky."

"That I did," confirmed Jonas. "There was a great big, bright light in the sky and the shape of it like an angel bigger than the world. And I heard a voice. . . ."

"We all saw the light," declared the first man. "And we all heard distinctly that voice from the sky."

"What did the voice say?" asked Joseph.

"It told us not to be afraid."

"Yes. It always begins that way. And then?"

"And then it said it brought us great news. The Savior of the world was being born. I remember the very words; how can I ever forget

them? 'For this day is born to you a Savior who is Christ the Lord.' "

"Christ the Lord," whispered Joseph.

"Yes, friend. That's what the voice said. It told us the child was being born right here in this town and that we would find it, wrapped in swaddling clothes and lying in a manger."

Another shepherd pushed himself forward.

"You can never imagine what happened then," he broke in excitedly. "The whole heaven seemed to open up. The curtain of the stars was split like a tent, and through the opening we saw a host of angels that filled the sky, and they were all singing at the top of their voices."

"And do you know what they were singing?" demanded Jonas, again interrupting. "The words were: 'Glory to God in the highest and on earth peace. . . .' " And then the shepherds seemed to lose their tongues. The sound of their own story seemed to subdue them. Strong outdoorsmen who smelled of grass—practical men—and yet they had told the story with something of the frenzy of poets. Now came the reaction.

Their leader lowered his lantern and sighed deeply. "Of course," he said with in apologetic air, "we can't expect you to believe all this."

Then his eyes flashed open and he looked straight at Joseph. "But it is true," he averred, as if he were taking an oath, "I saw it. I heard it."

Joseph wrung their hands. He believed them utterly, as they went on to tell how they forsook their fat-tailed sheep and ran into Bethlehem. Of every dark straggler on the streets at such in hour they had asked questions. Where could they find the newborn baby? And when they found this house then they must know if it were lying in a manger. Someone had sent them to the stable of the inn.

The tale of the shepherds brought peace to Joseph. The sign had come secondhand, which was better. These men, panting and out of breath and sweaty, full of strength and humility, had seen the gates of another world open up and had heard singing from on high, the heavens rejoicing at the birth of Mary's child. Humble workingmen of the fields were the first to come and visit the newborn Jesus.

Joseph received them with open arms and one shepherd after another kissed his beard. On tiptoe they followed him as he led them straight to the manger, where they looked down and then knelt beside the sleeping figure of Mary's son.

Soon they were gone, and Joseph resumed his unsleeping vigil. But now his heart was calmed. The sign had come. In his mind's ear he could hear the unnumbered hosts of the servants of God, singing to the ages, "Peace on earth to men of good will."

THE HOLY NIGHT

SELMA LAGERLOF

There was a man who went out in the dark night to borrow live coals to kindle a fire. He went from hut to hut and knocked. "Dear friends, help me!" said he. "My wife has just given birth to a child, and I must make a fire to warm her and the little one." But it was way in the night, and all the people were asleep. No one replied.

The man walked and walked. At last he saw the gleam of a fire a long way off. Then he went in that direction, and saw that the fire was burning in the open. A lot of sheep were sleeping around the fire, and an old shepherd sat and watched over the flock.

When the man who wanted to borrow fire came up to the sheep, he saw that three big dogs lay asleep at the shepherd's feet. All three awoke when the man approached and opened their great jaws, as though they wanted to bark; but not a sound was heard. The man noticed that the hair on their backs stood up and that their sharp, white teeth glistened in the firelight. They dashed toward him.

He felt that one of them bit at his leg and one at his hand and that one clung to his throat. But their jaws and teeth wouldn't obey them, and the man didn't suffer the least harm.

Now the man wished to go farther, to get what he needed. But the sheep lay so close to one another that he couldn't pass them. Then the man stepped upon their backs and walked over them and up to the fire. And not one of the animals awoke or moved.

When the man had almost reached the fire, the shepherd looked up. He was a surly old man, who was unfriendly and harsh toward human beings. And when he saw the strange man coming, he seized the long, spiked staff, which he always held in his hand when he tended his flock, and threw it at him. The staff came right toward the man, but, before it reached him, it turned off to one side and whizzed past him, far out in the meadow.

Now the man came up to the shepherd and said to him, "Good man, help me, and lend me a little fire! My wife has just given birth to a child, and I must make a fire to warm her and the little one."

The shepherd would rather have said no, but when he pondered that the dogs couldn't hurt the man, and the sheep had not run from him, and that the staff had not wished to strike him, he was a little afraid, and dared not deny the man that which he asked.

"Take as much as you need!" he said to the man. But then the fire was nearly burnt out. There were no logs or branches left, only a big heap of live coals; and the stranger

Peace on Earth

had neither spade nor shovel wherein he could carry the red-hot coals. When the shepherd saw this, he said again, "Take as much as you need!" He was glad that the man wouldn't be able to take away any coals.

But the man stooped and picked coals from the ashes with his bare hands, and laid them in his mantle. And he didn't burn his hands when he touched them, nor did the coals scorch his mantle; but he carried them away as if they had been nuts or apples.

And when the shepherd, who was such a cruel and hardhearted man, saw all this, he began to wonder to himself: What kind of a night is this, when the dogs do not bite, the sheep are not scared, the staff does not kill, or the fire scorch? He called the stranger back and said to him, "What kind of a night is this? And how does it happen that all things show you compassion?"

Then said the man, "I cannot tell you if you yourself do not see it." And he wished to go his way, that he might soon make a fire and warm his wife and child.

But the shepherd did not wish to lose sight of the man before he had found out what all this might portend. He got up and followed the man till they came to the place where he lived. Then the shepherd saw that the man didn't have so much as a hut to dwell in, but that his wife and babe were lying in a mountain grotto, where there was nothing except the cold and naked stone walls.

But the shepherd thought that perhaps the poor innocent child might freeze to death there in the grotto; and, although he was a hard man, he was touched and thought he would like to help it. And he loosened his knapsack from his

WITH JOYF
CHRISTMA

WISHES

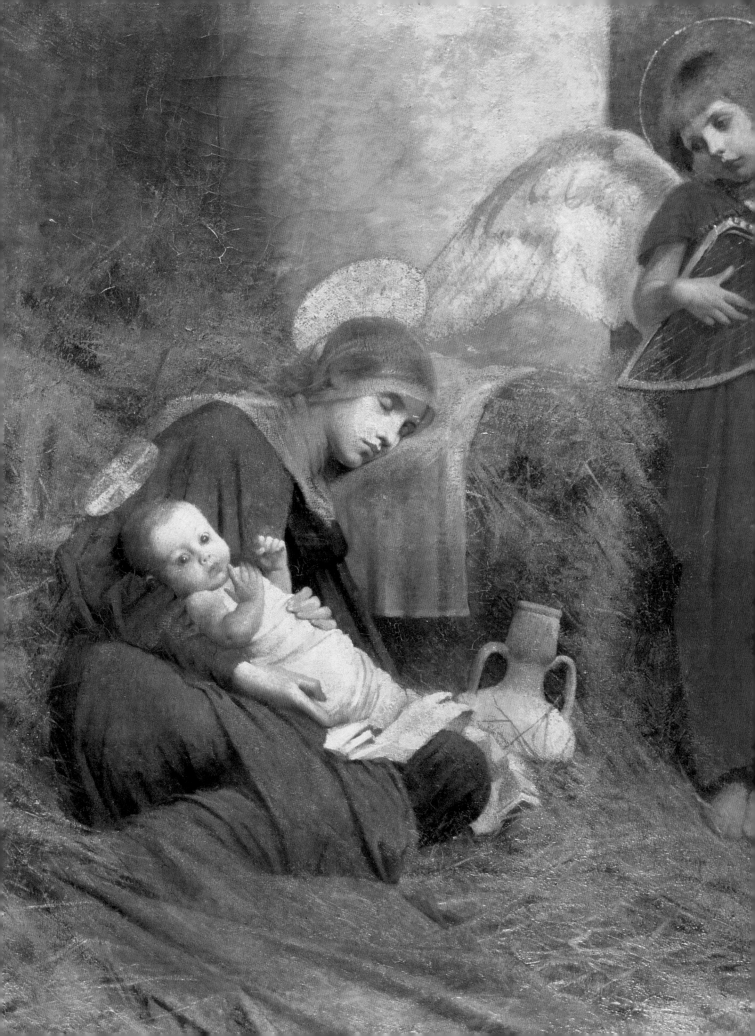

shoulder, took from it a soft white sheepskin, gave it to the strange man, and said that he should let the child sleep on it.

But just as soon as he showed that he, too, could be merciful, his eyes were opened; and he saw what he had not been able to see before and heard what he could not have heard before.

He saw that all around him stood a ring of little silver-winged angels and each held a stringed instrument and all sang in loud tones that tonight the Savior was born who should redeem the world from its sins. Then he understood how all things were so happy this night that they didn't want to do anything wrong.

And it was not only around the shepherd that there were angels, but he saw them everywhere. They sat inside the grotto, they sat outside on the mountain, and they flew under the heavens. They came marching in great companies, and as they passed they paused and cast a glance at the child.

There was such jubilation and such gladness and songs and play! And all this he saw in the dark night, whereas before he could not have made out anything. He was so happy because his eyes had been opened that he fell upon his knees and thanked God.

What that shepherd saw, we might also see, for the angels fly down from heaven every Christmas Eve, if we could only see them.

You must remember this, for it is as true, as true as that I see you and you see me. It is not revealed by the light of lamps or candles, and it does not depend upon sun and moon; but that which is needful is that we have such eyes as can see God's glory.

TROUBLE AT THE INN

DINA DONOHUE

For years now, whenever Christmas pageants are talked about, in a certain little town in the Midwest, someone is sure to mention the name of Wallace Purling. Wally's performance in one annual production of the Nativity play has slipped into the realm of legend. But the old-timers who were in the audience that night never tire of recalling exactly what happened.

Wally was nine that year and in the second grade, though he should have been in the fourth. Most people in town knew that he had difficulty in keeping up. He was big and clumsy, slow in movement and mind. Still, Wally was well liked by the other children in his class, all of whom were smaller than he, though the boys had trouble hiding their irritation if the uncoordinated Wally asked to play ball with them.

Most often they'd find a way to keep him off the field, but Wally would hang around anyway—not sulking, just hoping. He was always a helpful boy, a willing and smiling one, and the natural protector, paradoxically, of the underdog. Sometimes if the older boys chased the younger ones away, it would always be Wally who'd say, "Can't they stay? They're no bother."

Wally fancied the idea of being a shepherd with a flute in the Christmas pageant that year, but the play's director, Miss Lumbard, assigned him to a more important role. After all, she reasoned, the Innkeeper did not have too many lines, and Wally's size would make his refusal of lodging to Joseph more forceful.

And so it happened that the usual large, partisan audience gathered for the town's Yuletide extravaganza of the staffs and créches, of beards, crowns, halos and a whole stage full of squeaky voices. No one onstage or off was more caught up in the magic of the night than Wallace Purling. They said later that he stood in the wings and watched the performance with such fascination that from time to time Miss Lumbard had to make sure he didn't wander onstage before his cue.

Then the time came when Joseph appeared, slowly, tenderly guiding Mary to the door of the inn. Joseph knocked hard on the wooden door set into the painted backdrop. Wally the Innkeeper was there, waiting. "What do you want?" Wally said, swinging the door open with a brusque gesture.

"We seek lodging."

"Seek it elsewhere." Wally looked straight ahead but spoke vigorously. "The inn is filled."

"Sir, we have asked everywhere in vain. We have traveled far and are very weary."

"There is no room in this inn for you." Wally looked properly stern.

"Please, good innkeeper, this is my wife, Mary. She is heavy with child and needs a place to rest. Surely you must have some small corner for her. She is so tired."

For the first time, the Innkeeper relaxed his stiff stance and looked down at Mary. With that, there was a long pause, long enough to make the audience a bit tense with embarrassment.

"No! Begone!" the prompter whispered from the wings.

"No!" Wally repeated automatically. "Begone!"

Joseph sadly placed his arm around Mary, and Mary laid her head upon his shoulder, and the two of them started to move away. The Innkeeper did not return inside his inn, however. Wally stood there in the doorway, watching the forlorn couple. His mouth was open, his brow creased with concern, his eyes filling unmistakably with tears.

"Don't go, Joseph," Wally called out. "Bring Mary back." And Wallace Purling's face grew into a bright smile. "You can have my room."

Some people in town thought that the pageant had been ruined. Yet there were others—many others—who considered it the most Christmas of all Christmas pageants they had ever seen.

THE GOSPEL STORY

And it came to pass in those days, that there went out a decree from Caesar Augustus, that all the world should be taxed. (And this taxing was first made when Cyrenius was governor of Syria.) And all went to be taxed, every one into his own city.

And Joseph also went up from Galilee, out of the city of Nazareth, into Judaea, unto the city of David, which is called Bethlehem; (because he was of the house and lineage of David:) To be taxed with Mary his espoused wife, being great with child.

And so it was, that, while they were there, the days were accomplished that she should be delivered. And she brought forth her firstborn son, and wrapped him in swaddling clothes, and laid him in a manger; because there was no room for them in the inn.

And there were in the same country shepherds abiding in the field, keeping watch over their flock by night. And, lo, the angel of the Lord came upon them, and the glory of the Lord shone round about them: and they were sore afraid.

And the angel said unto them, Fear not: for, behold, I bring you good tidings of great joy, which shall be to all people. For unto you is born this day in the city of David a Saviour, which is Christ the Lord. And this shall be a sign unto you; Ye shall find the babe wrapped in swaddling clothes, lying in a manger.

And suddenly there was with the angel a multitude of the heavenly host praising God, and saying, Glory to God in the highest, and on earth peace, good will toward men. And it came to pass, as the angels were gone away from them into heaven, the shepherds said one to another, Let us now go even unto Bethlehem, and see this thing which is come to pass, which the Lord hath made known unto us.

And they came with haste, and found Mary, and Joseph, and the babe lying in a manger. And when they had seen it, they made known abroad the saying which was told them concerning this child. And all they that heard it wondered at those things which were told them by the shepherds. But Mary kept all these things, and pondered them in her heart.

And the shepherds returned, glorifying and praising God for all the things that they had heard and seen, as it was told unto them.

INDEX